Heaven C

Little One (1994)

HEAVEN CAN COME LATER

Ann Walker

ARROW

This edition published by Arrow Books Ltd 1996

2 4 6 8 10 9 7 5 3 1

First published in the United Kingdom in 1989 by
Excalibur Press, London

Arrow Book Ltd
Random House, 20 Vauxhall Bridge Road, London SW1V 2SA

Random House Australia (Pty) Limited
16 Dalmore Drive, Scoresby,
Victoria 3179, Australia

Random House New Zealand Limited
18 Poland Road, Glenfield,
Auckland 10, New Zealand

Random House South Africa (Pty) Limited
PO Box 2263, Rosebank 2121, South Africa

Random House UK Limited Reg. No. 954009

A CIP catalogue record for this book
is available from the British Library

ISBN 0 09 942721 4

Papers used by Random House UK Ltd are natural, recyclable
products made from wood grown in sustainable forests. The
manufacturing processes conform to the environmental regulations of
the country of origin

Typeset in 10/11 Ehrhardt Sabon by
Palimpsest Book Production Limited,
Polmont, Stirlingshire

Printed and bound in Great Britain by
BPC Paperbacks Ltd
a member of The British Printing Company Ltd

Introduction

This is the true story of my life, and I have written it to show people that no matter how life treats them, whether it be good or bad, we each have a friend in the spirit world called a spirit guide. He or she is with us for a lifetime and even during our darkest hours is right by our side. It is also to show that not only do we have guides, or as some people call them, guardian angels, we also always have with us our families and loved ones, who have gone to 'spirit'.

I believe everybody has a guide to help them through life and this book is simply about my life before and after I met my spirit guide, White Arrow.

I dedicate it, in reverence, to the cherished support and unselfish patience of my family, without which this book could not have been written. This book also could not have been possible without the help of my friend Valerie Smith, who gave me the inspiration and desire to start it, help with writing it and the courage to finish it.

Chapter 1

It was 11 September 1942. England was at war with Germany and as bombs were being dropped over England, so many new babies were being born. One of these newborn infants came into the world in Clacton-on-Sea in the early hours of the morning. There were many new babies being born at this time and it was everyone's dream that this new generation would be filled with hope and the ability to bring peace to our troubled world.

A young girl of twenty-two was being wheeled into a maternity hospital. She was quite an attractive woman with fair hair. With the onset of labour she was anxious about the safe arrival of her baby which she hoped wouldn't be too long. She sat patiently in the wheelchair as she waited for the nursing staff to wheel her into the small, stark but sterile delivery room. The nurse said, 'Don't worry, love, everything will be just fine. Sit there for a moment whilst I prepare the delivery table for you.' She smiled at the young mother-to-be, only to be stopped in her tracks.

'I'm sorry, nurse,' said the young woman, 'but I don't think I can wait any longer. I'm sure the baby's nearly there because I want to push!' She was trying not to make a fuss but it was obvious there was very little time to waste. The nurse immediately stopped what she was doing in order to examine her.

'Yes, you're quite right, love. The baby's head's nearly there! Don't worry, I won't leave you, but I'll ring for the doctor to come at once.'

She pressed the bell and within seconds the doctor appeared. 'This lady is well into the second stage,' he said to the nurse. 'We'll have to act fast. Let's get her on to the delivery table. I'm afraid we'll have to forget about the other deliveries for the time being. There's no time to lose.'

They had just managed to lift the young woman on to the table when the head emerged. The nurse said 'Breathe deeply, my dear, and as soon as the doctor says you can push, push with all your might.' A baby girl was born.

As I lay in my mother's arms, little did she and I know that another war was about to break out. The one I had chosen to experience was to last thirty-seven years. The reason why I had made that choice was to come to light many years later.

At this precious moment, however, there was only one thing my mother was interested in and that was her new daughter. She already had a young son, but, as she held me tightly to her bosom, she realised she had always wanted a fair-haired, blue-eyed girl.

My father was stationed in the army at Clacton-on-Sea, hence my birth place. My mother had no visitors the day I was born because Dad was in the army prison. He had been caught trying to desert. He was only twenty-three or twenty-four years old and at least six feet tall with dark hair, a very good-looking man. He was also an alcoholic. My mother suffered two miscarriages altogether, one before my brother was born and then another before I came along. On each occasion the loss of the unborn babies had been due to my father's violence. My mother must have had a tremendous sense of relief to have succeeded in giving birth to both a son and a daughter.

Dad came from a very poor Welsh family and was brought up during the Depression. His mother died when I was only about one or two years old, so I don't have many recollections of her. According to those who knew her, she went out one evening and dropped dead in the street from a heart attack. Apparently my father didn't attend her funeral, for his drink was far more important to him.

Mum was only nineteen when she met and fell in love with my Dad. He was always immaculately dressed and never left the house without combing his hair first or polishing his shoes. Very soon after they met, Mum became pregnant. In those days it was regarded as shameful to be pregnant outside marriage. Mum was well aware of Dad's drink problem, which had started since he left his native Wales, and she actually went to consult a member of her family as to whether she should go ahead and marry him. She was told to go ahead, if not for him, for the sake of the child she was carrying. Personally, I believe Mum was fated to marry him.

Mum hoped their first child would be able to bring change and fresh hope into his life, but she had her first miscarriage. Very soon she became pregnant again and this time successfully gave birth to Raymond, my brother, in June 1940. My father became more and more drunk and was violent not only to my mother but to his young child, too. By the time Raymond reached his second year he was totally deaf and dumb. The doctors said it was due to my brother having fallen from his high chair, getting his leg caught in it in the process, but my relatives had seen my father hit my brother around the ears and head many a time. I only hope to God the doctors were right – but I doubt if anyone will ever know the truth.

During my early years I hardly saw anything of my brother, mainly because he was in and out of hospital all the time, so my memory of him at a young age is very limited. I do remember, however, that we never seemed to stay for long in one place and were always on the move. By the time I was about five I vaguely recollect there being gaps when I saw neither my mother nor my father, and I think this was because I was put into care from time to time when my mother couldn't find adequate shelter for the two of us. Being so young, my memory of this soon faded, although it went on until I reached the age of eight when I was more capable of understanding what was going on. Around this time I can clearly remember getting ready for school one morning. I was eating a slice of toast and having a cup of tea for my breakfast when Mum called to me. I loved her so much and she always gave me a kiss and a cuddle before I left for school in the mornings. This particular day, however, she seemed upset and it looked to me as if she had been crying because her eyes were very red. She squeezed me so tightly I could hardly breathe and she said, 'I love you, Ann.'

'I love you, too,' I replied, wondering what all the extra attention I was receiving was about – not that I didn't enjoy it! The trouble was, I was running a bit behind schedule and was due to meet my friend on the corner before we set off for school, so I quickly gave her a hug back and, after kissing her on the cheek, I rushed out saying my goodbyes in the typical fashion of any normal eight-year-old. Half of me would have longed to have stayed at home with Mum and for that lovely cuddle not to finish and to stay in her arms. I was too young to sense anything was very wrong, not even when Mum came rushing out behind me, repeating loudly that she loved me and to be careful. I assured her I loved her too and and, after promising to be careful, I gave Mum a wave and walked towards my friend who was already at the street corner waiting for me. We were in the same class at school and arrived together nice and early that morning. When we went into our classroom we mucked about, throwing books at each other and chasing each other around the desks. I was always happy at school and enjoyed my lessons. I was also beginning to realise the unhappiness my father was causing the family, so in a way I felt safe at school. My friend and I sat next to each other in class and we still had mischief on our minds as the first lesson began. We were giggling and passing to each other little bits of paper with silly notes scribbled on them.

Suddenly the classroom door opened and in walked the headmistress. We all sat in silence as she spoke in private to the class teacher. After the teacher had received her instructions she called out, 'Ann Pinkham, will you go with Miss Edwards to her office, please.'

I pushed my chair back saying, 'Yes, miss,' and walked out of the classroom behind the headmistress. Miss Edwards was a very strict woman in her forties who usually wore grey or tweed suits and brogue shoes. She wore, too, her greying hair in a bun, which made her look even more severe. She told me there were two ladies waiting to meet me and showed me into her office. I had never set eyes on the women before. I was told to sit down on the chair and Miss Edwards had a brief conversation with them which went over my head. I wasn't really interested in what they were saying, being anxious in getting back to my classroom and my friend. After a couple of minutes I started to feel bored and began to kick my legs from front to back, knocking the back of the chair with my shoes.

One of the strangers turned and smiled at me, but I didn't like her and glanced the other way, tossing my head.

'Stop that, Ann,' said Miss Edwards.

I looked up and apologised, after which the three women carried on talking. Eventually, the headmistress got up from her desk and said, 'Ann,' as she walked towards me, 'you will have to leave with these ladies, as they will be taking you to a new home.'

I immediately thought to myself, Oh, Mum, where are you? I said and did nothing for a moment, but then looked towards the door and started to run for it. It would only take me five minutes to run home to Mum and she would stop them taking me anywhere, I thought. I didn't get far before one of the strangers grabbed me by the arm.

'No, Ann, you have to come with us, I'm afraid,' she said, and promptly sat me back on the chair. 'It's no use trying to run away, you have to come with us and that's all there is to it.'

I could feel the tears slowly building up but I was adamant they wouldn't see me cry so I took it out on the chair legs again by banging my shoes against the chair. This time no one said anything to stop me. They whispered something between themselves and then one of the ladies walked towards me and said, 'Come on, Ann. Let's go.'

I was afraid so I leant back in my chair, frightened to move or speak. I wanted my Mum. I was terrified. The woman grabbed hold of my hand and pulled me up, then started walking to the door, with me dragging my feet behind. I knew I had no choice but to go, but I had no idea where we were going and that really frightened me. We got outside the school gates where a parked car was waiting for us. The other lady had caught up with us and unlocked the car door whilst the first one, still holding my hand, pushed me gently into the back of the car.

The women both got in and spoke quietly to each other. I could see my classroom from where I was sitting and wondered if I would ever see my friend again and if she would miss me. My main worry though was, naturally, what would my Mum say? As I looked out of the car window I said to myself, Please, Mum, come and get me. You wouldn't let these strangers take me away, would you? Please, Mum, do something. Then I couldn't contain my despair any more. The great big lump in my throat seemed to explode and I cried uncontrollably.

The car started and we set off. As we passed the houses and buildings we went past my own house. I got up on my knees to look out of the back window, hoping I would see Mum. The tears were streaming down my cheeks as I looked at our front door. There was no sign of Mum, nothing at all and, as the car gathered speed, the house began to fade out of focus until I could see it no more. I sat back down on the back seat and cried out, 'I want my Mum. I don't want to go with you,' and I leant against the car door. With that, the car came to a grinding halt, making me fall to the floor. The woman in the passenger seat got out of the car and got into the back next to me. By this time I was really sobbing, thinking the end of the world had come, for they were taking me away from my Mum and I didn't know if I would ever see her again.

The woman sitting next to me changed her attitude and for the first time showed some compassion. She held me close and said softly, 'Come on, love, you'll see your Mum soon. It won't be long, I promise.'

Very soon after that I cried myself to sleep, propped up against the lady. I woke up some time later with a start when the car had stopped. I rubbed my eyes and sat up straight to look out of the car window. All I could see was a large building in front of us. From an eight-year-old child's viewpoint it looked like a castle, but it was in fact a convent called St Ann's. We had driven all the way to Orpington in Kent, miles away from my home and my Mum.

Chapter 2

We got out of the car and the two women took me inside the convent. It was all so bewildering to me. I couldn't understand why my Mum wasn't there waiting for me or why I had been taken there at all. The three of us sat in a room until a nun came in. Once again they all spoke to each other quietly, completely ignoring me. After a little while the two women left and I was now alone with the nun. I was more scared of her than I was of the two women. 'Come along with me, Ann,' she said and we went along some corridors until we came to a large room. I later learned it was called a dormitory and there were eight beds in it. When the two women had arrived at my school to take me away with them they had with them a small suitcase. The sister showed me which of the beds would be mine and told me to unpack the suitcase. She told me she would return in ten minutes to take me to the dining room and introduce me to the other children.

I was soon to learn that the convent was a place where children from similar backgrounds to mine were sent. Many of the children there were as unhappy as I was. I tried very hard to resign myself to the fact that I might as well make the most of my situation, but although I got on well with the children and the nuns, I was never truly happy being away from Mum.

I was at the convent for about eighteen months. I was ten years old when one day, I was sitting in my classroom having a lesson with all the other children, and once again I was summoned to go to the office. This time the headmistress was called Mother Superior. I sat outside her office, wondering what I had done wrong. I could hear voices coming from inside the room and I could tell the Mother Superior was speaking to another woman.

Suddenly, the door opened and Mother Superior came out

into the corridor. 'Ann,' she said, 'please come inside, will you?' Mother Superior had such a lovely kind voice. 'There is somebody here who would very much like to see you,' she smiled sweetly.

I got up from the chair and stood still for a moment, remembering the last time I had found myself in a similar situation. What was to happen to me this time? I wondered. Mother Superior looked at me almost as if she could read my mind because she said, 'Go in and don't be afraid, Little One. You'll be so happy when you know what this is all about.'

Years later I was to be referred to as 'Little One', but by a different source.

I opened the door tentatively and as it swung back I saw Mum sitting on a chair right in front of me. I couldn't move. After all this time I was with my mother once more. The tears flowed freely as I stood there, hardly daring to blink in case I was dreaming. Mum was crying also and got up with her arms outstretched. 'Ann, darling,' she cried, and I rushed into them, longing for them to hug me. No words were uttered, no words were necessary. Instead we just held each other tightly. Mum 'Come on, love. I'm taking you home now.'

I looked up at her to make sure she really meant it. I loved her so much, but I had to ask that burning, nagging question which had been eating away at me, 'You won't leave me again, will you, Mum?'

She hugged me tight, saying reassuringly, 'No, darling, I promise, I promise.'

One of the nuns brought my belongings and Mum and I walked out of the office clinging on to each other. The Mother Superior was still outside in the corridor and as we came out she shook Mum's hand and smiled at me, wishing us both all the very best. I said my goodbyes and we walked out of the convent and into the sunlight, one of the most wonderful moments of my life.

It was a gloriously sunny day and I felt so happy. From a very early age I had learnt not to ask Mum many questions about her and Dad, and I wasn't going to start now. I was just relieved and delighted to be with her. We walked to the bus-stop, and on the way home Mum asked me to tell her all about the convent and what the people there were like. She asked if I was worried about anything, if there was anything at all I was to discuss it with her. For a ten-year-old I was a deep-thinking child, and maybe growing up too fast, but I knew I had to somehow convince Mum I was fine.

We got off the bus at the top of our road. No sooner had we gone a few yards when Mum suddenly grabbed hold of my hand. I looked around me to find out what had startled her and in the distance I could see my father walking towards us. Mum continued to hold my hand tightly and we walked towards him. I suppose I had missed my dad in a strange way and was pleased to see him. As he approached us all he said, however, was 'Hello,' and started talking to Mum, completely ignoring me. We all went home together and as the day went by it was as if nothing had really changed since I was at last at home with them both. They were still shouting at each other. When I went to bed that night I could hear them arguing as they had always done, but somehow it didn't matter. I was with my mum now and, hopefully, nothing was going to change that.

I was older now and I was more aware of the beatings and abuse my father was giving my mother – and now I was hating him for it. I found that whenever Dad entered the room I would go out of the room and into my bedroom, for I knew if I had stayed he would start picking on me too and I couldn't face that. On numerous occasions when Dad was polishing his shoes he'd start a row with me and if the answers I came up with didn't suit him, he would hit me with the shoe across my head or face.

After a year or so we moved to West Harrow to a lovely big flat and at this stage my brother came home to live with us, after living in a hospital and then special schools for the deaf and dumb. I was so pleased to have my brother living at home. I knew he couldn't hear the beatings and foul language my father used. I was twelve years old and the next couple of years were extremely difficult to get through. Whether it was because I was becoming an adolescent and the changes in my body were affecting me, or whether I was becoming more aware of what was happening I don't really know, but it was probably a combination of the two. One thing I was certain about was that I couldn't bear to see Mum suffering the continuous beatings and verbal abuse she was receiving from Dad. Time and time again I ran away from home during these years but the police always managed to find me and take me back. I was making Mum even more unhappy by running away, but I couldn't stand seeing her distressed and frightened all the time. The trouble was, there didn't appear to be a solution to it all, as we were both too scared of Dad to do anything.

Those awful times left a scar on me which lasted many years. There was one particular night, a typical night which sums up what it was like at home. I had been watching television that evening with Mum when suddenly she said to me, 'You'd better go to bed now, Ann, your Dad'll be in soon.'

I sensed urgency in her voice and knew my father was due to come in at any time. I was used to this so I kissed Mum good night, hoping she would be all right. That night I went to bed forgetting to put the wardrobe behind my bedroom door, and Mum called out to remind me to do so. After I had moved it into position, I sat on my bed and stared at it, thinking, good, no one would be able to push the door open, and then I got into bed.

I took a book from the dressing table and started to read it. I was deeply engrossed in the story when suddenly I heard Dad come in. I put the book down and slid beneath the bedclothes, hoping that everyone would have a quiet, good night – a quiet, good night meant all the shouting and bawling would be over and done with in ten minutes. I heard Mum ask Dad if he wanted anything to eat and by this time I felt sick – I always did, night after night – never knowing if it was to be a good night or not. I heard Dad moving about in the front room and call out to Mum, 'Yes, Letty, I wouldn't mind a sandwich.' He sounded fairly amicable and in a good mood. Great, I thought, and grabbed one of my pillows and put it over my head. I had been reading a love story and as I was trying to get off to sleep, I was in a sort of day-dream, remembering the lovely story.

All of a sudden, I heard an almighty scream. Fear brought tears to my eyes. Every night, when I went to bed, I always thought that I wouldn't be able to cry any more or experience fear within me any more, but once again it was happening. As I had always done, I tried to press the pillow against my ears so I couldn't hear the shouting and crying, but it made no difference. I could still hear the slaps and the punches and Mum's screams. I took the pillow away from my head when I realised there was no point in it being there. I desperately wanted to help Mum. I hated him so much but I had to live by Mum's words of warning.

'You'll only make it worse for me, Ann. If you get hurt I just couldn't stand it.'

I hated everything and everyone, except for Mum of course. Why her and why me? What had we done to deserve such treatment?

I got out of bed and went towards the wall which was next to the front room. I put my ear as close to it as possible, wanting to know Mum was safe. Suddenly, all went quiet for a few seconds, apart from Mum sobbing very softly. I thought it must all be over. I could hear Dad going into the kitchen, and then I heard a scraping, dragging noise. I couldn't make out what the noise was. Then I heard him coming back, trying to open the door between the kitchen and the front room. There was obviously something obstructing his way, something which was preventing him opening the door, but I didn't know what. All went quiet again and the deathly silence scared me but I daren't move in case I made a noise.

Just then, Dad called out to Mum, 'Letty, open the door.'

'No!' I heard Mum say.

'Please, I won't hurt you, I promise,' said Dad.

I was still standing there, not daring to move in case he heard me. I was praying for Mum not open the door, when

I heard her call out, 'Tom, I'm sitting on the windowsill. If you push open the door, I'll jump!'

I thought to myself, My God, am I hearing things?

Dad tried different tactics and this time tried to soften the tone in his voice. He said, 'Open the door, Letty. I love you. I promise if you just let me in I won't hurt you. Please, Letty, love.'

By this time I was crying softly, hoping Dad wouldn't hear in case it made matters worse. I went over to my bed and lay down, putting the pillow partly over my head, hoping that no one could hear my sobbing, and trying to hear Mum's reply at the same time.

She said, 'If you come in, Tom, I'll jump.'

'Oh, please don't do that, Mum,' I said to myself quietly. 'I love you.'

Then I heard my Dad speak again, still in his wickedly enticing way. 'Letty, I love you more than anything. You know I didn't mean to hurt you.' I've heard it all before, Dad, I thought, you can be so devious when you want to be. And I prayed Mum wouldn't open that door.

Dad continued to call out to Mum, pleading with her to let him in. I could never, and definitely would never, trust him nor his sweet talking, so I pulled my pillow closer over my ears, terrified for Mum's safety.

After a couple of minutes I could hear the scraping, dragging sound again. I thought to myself, No, no Mum, please don't. I knew that whatever it was she had put behind the door, she was now removing it because she believed Dad's pie-crust promises. Even at my young age I knew my father better than she did.

'Tom . . .' I heard her cry, but it was too late, within a split second there was an almighty scream and then more screams. It went on for a good ten minutes, but it seemed a lifetime to me, so God knows how long it seemed to my poor mother.

After the screaming came the long silence. All I could hear was my father walking to the bathroom and then towards the bedroom. I couldn't hear my Mum at all and I didn't know whether she was dead or alive. She had always told me never to come out of my room, whatever happened, until she told me to, so I cried myself to sleep instead. I couldn't get the screaming out of my mind. It was the worst experience I had been through and hatred for my father was so deeply rooted in me that I never forgave him, from that day on.

The following morning I woke up, still not knowing if Mum was alive or not. I got myself ready for school and after a while thought I could hear her out in the kitchen. Yes, thank God! I rushed out of my bedroom towards the kitchen to Mum, who had her back to me. Dad must have already left for work and she was cooking my breakfast.

I said, with a cry in my voice, 'Oh Mum, thank God you're all right. I was so frightened after what happened last night.'

She slowly turned round to face me and I saw for the first time the injuries she had sustained. Her face was black and blue and one eye was so swollen it had doubled in size. There was a look on her face as if she wanted to cry but couldn't because it hurt so much. How could a man get away with it? Why should it be allowed? I asked myself as I looked at her, but what could I do? It was the first time I had seen my mother's face so badly beaten up, and it was to leave an emotional scar on me for the rest of my life. At only thirty-six years old, my mother had suffered more brutal kicks, punches and physical and mental cruelty than most people witness in a whole lifetime.

After that dreadful night, things went from bad to worse. I kept running away and the authorities eventually made me a ward of court. They allowed me to stay with Mum and Dad, but only because they were aware of the close bond between my mother and me. By the time I reached fourteen and a half I left school. I had made good friends with a girl called Sheila and spent most of my time round at her house until in the end her family suggested that I leave home and move in with them. Mum agreed to this, and then she and Dad moved. They didn't tell me what their new address was and I felt very guilty for leaving her alone with Dad. Raymond had also left home to live with friends of his.

Chapter 3

As Sheila and I had left school and neither of us had a job, we had plenty of time on our hands which we spent hanging around in cafés in Harrow. One day I was feeling down in the dumps, wishing I knew how Mum was and where they were living.

'I'll tell you what will cheer you up and get you to stop thinking about your parents,' said Sheila, jumping up from her chair with excitement. She produced a tube of pills from her handbag, telling me they were supposed to cheer people up when they were depressed or worried about something. She said, 'I've never tried them myself, but I bought some because I've been told they're really good. Anyway, what harm will it do just to try a couple?' Why not? I thought to myself and so we shared the pills between us. There were twenty pills in the tube so we had ten each. The following morning we both felt terribly ill. They had certainly made me feel carefree and safe for the first time in my life. I enjoyed that feeling but didn't want to take any more and neither did Sheila, so we decided not to do it again.

Although Sheila was a good friend and her parents were kind to me, I was beginning to miss my own home and family. Blood is thicker than water and nobody, but nobody, can ever take the place of your mother. One day I decided it would make an enjoyable day out to visit my mother's youngest sister, Shirley. Her real name was Ruth, but my mother had started to call her Shirley at a young age because she had such lovely, fair curly hair, like Shirley Temple's, and the nickname stuck for the rest of her life. She suggested I should come and live with her, my Uncle George and my cousins Joyce and David. I felt this would be a step in the right direction and so I said my thank yous and farewells to Sheila and her family and went to live with my relatives.

It was the next best thing to live with Mum's sister as I couldn't live with Mum herself. They treated me well and I soon found myself a job in a paint factory, trying my best to live a normal life. In spite of all my hard efforts to find peace, however, I was still not entirely happy, simply because Mum wasn't there, and I missed her very much.

My aunt and uncle were towers of strength. They stressed time and time again that Mum was completely terrified of Dad, and they told me more about Dad's appalling behaviour towards my mother, keeping nothing from me. Dad had even broken my mother's shoulder during one of his fits of temper. I asked them why on earth Mum had never left him and they said she had, on numerous occasions, but somehow or another Dad always managed to find out where she had gone and win her back with his devilish ways. In those days there were no such thing as shelter for battered wives so Mum really didn't have much choice but to put up with it, especially when I was around.

I had a probation officer who had to be kept informed of my whereabouts. She was aware that I had been living at Sheila's house and then with my aunt and uncle. When work at the factory became too monotonous for me, I asked my cousin Joyce if there was any chance of her getting me a job at her company, a baby clothing firm. Luckily she was able to and I enjoyed my work there a great deal. Joyce and I were the same age and, because the two of us were the eldest cousins in the family, we had been friends ever since I could remember. Nevertheless, I gradually found myself missing my mother more and more, but I still had no idea where she was living or what she was doing, nor indeed, what had been going on since I had left home. I tried desperately hard not to hurt my Uncle George's feelings, but one day I summoned up the courage to tell him how I was longing to get in touch with Mum.

'Ann, it is entirely up to you, love,' he said. 'We understand how you must feel. Both your aunt and I want what's best for you, just as long as you are happy. You must do what you think best.'

I was so glad they understood. You can't imagine how much that meant to me.

By now I was fifteen and a half. No one knew where Mum was and it seemed an impossible task to track her down. I was beginning to withdraw into myself, into a deep depression.

One day, during my lunch break, I went to the local parade of shops. I needed a chemist's because I had a terrible headache. As I waited to be served my eyes moved along the shelves. There in front of me were the pills I had tried that day with Sheila. As I stared at them I remembered the wonderful feeling they had given me, the sense of security and freedom.

When the assistant returned with the headache pills she asked me if there was anything else I wanted.

I said, 'No thank you, that's all,' and walked back to work.

All that afternoon I couldn't stop thinking about the 'magic' pills. It wouldn't do me any harm, surely, to try them once more. I just needed to feel everything was right with the world again, and this was the only way I could think of to create that illusion.

By the end of the afternoon I had talked myself into going straight back to the chemist after work. I walked in and bought a tube. I didn't take any of the pills straight away because I remembered how awful Sheila and I had both felt afterwards and the following morning I looked at the tube sitting on my lap, and I knew I'd be foolish to take them. Then I thought to myself, Yes, I'll just take a couple for now and see how it goes . . .

I felt sure that a couple would be sufficient, that I wouldn't get used to them, but how wrong I was. Within a month I was well and truly hooked. I wouldn't say I was happy taking them, but they helped me to cope with life and I felt I could take each day as it came along. The lift they gave me to overcome the pain I had been feeling for such a long time was incredible, and I was determined I wasn't going to be hurt any more. To me, the pills were my safeguard against life in general. They didn't appear to affect me in a way other people would notice, and somehow or other life carried on as if nothing was wrong; that is, until one day when my uncle and aunt asked to have a word with me. I had been careless at work and someone had seen me taking pills and had informed them. My aunt and uncle were not angry with me, surprisingly enough, but intensely worried. By this time I had no intention of giving the pills up. I told them a few lies and managed to convince them it wasn't as bad as they thought, but from that time on they kept a very careful watch over me.

Not long after that I made up my mind it would be best for me to leave. I told them I would go back to Sheila and her family for a while. I was coming up to sixteen now, and soon I would be too old to be a ward of court, but until then I had to tell my probation officer of my whereabouts.

I didn't stay long at Sheila's but moved in with some other friends the same age as me. They were all aware of my taking pills but all tried to help me stop taking them and see sense. Perhaps some of them guessed the reason I was taking drugs but, then again, we were all so young, reckless and, particularly in my case, mixed up, that escapism was a common answer to problems.

As time went by, the drugs began to make me feel very, very ill, although of course I would not admit that the pills were the cause.

One Friday, however, one of the friends I was living with came with me to town to go shopping. We had a good day out and, tired and weary, caught a bus back home. On the way I suddenly developed stomach pains so severe that they made me double up. They became so acute that the driver had to stop the bus and send for an ambulance. I was taken to Harrow on the Hill hospital, where two doctors examined me. I can still remember them arguing whether it would be better to keep me in overnight for observation or not. They were unaware I had been taking drugs, but decided that the pain was caused by acid which had formed in my stomach. They sent me home the next morning, saying that there was nothing they could do for me. That evening I still felt terribly ill. I tried to distract myself by meeting a group of friends at the Drop In Café in Harrow, but eventually I gave up pretending everything was fine and asked one of my friends if I could possibly sleep in the back of his car until I felt a bit better.

When I woke up I found that he had driven me back to the hospital. The lady doctor whom I had seen when I first collapsed arranged for me to be admitted for observation, deciding to keep me in that Saturday night. I still don't know how the doctors managed to do it, but miraculously they were able to find my mother. I had been resting for a couple of days and was feeling a little better when the sister told me I had a visitor. I thanked her and sat up in bed, preening myself ready to receive my mystery visitor. I looked up and there she was: Mum was standing next to my bed. We fell into each other's arms, cuddled each other and cried. I felt like pinching myself to make sure it was really happening. We had so much to catch up on.

She said that Dad had recently discovered her latest address and was back living with her, so she wouldn't be able to stay with me too long. I looked into her eyes and could see the fear inside her. Although she loved me, the fear she had of my father was so great that she felt she had to get back before he realised she had gone out. She was only a young woman herself, and when I saw the terror and pain she was experiencing I made up my mind there and then that I couldn't and wouldn't let her endure any more suffering. The time had come for something to be done once and for all. She gave me her address and I promised to see her very soon. We kissed each other goodbye and I squeezed her as I cuddled her. She blew me another kiss and then waved as she reached the door, and after she'd gone I lay back on my pillow. I knew I had to do everything within my power to ensure she wouldn't have to suffer any more. I was the only person who could help her. I resolved to go and face my father.

I was discharged from hospital the following evening, and the next day I went along to meet Mum after she had finished work. This pattern continued for the next month or so. It was so good for us both to see each other again. Meeting her this way meant Dad knew nothing of what was going on. Finally I went to confront my father at their home whilst Mum was there. Six months previously I had had a tattoo engraved on my arm with the word 'MUM'. My father straight away caught sight of it. He had obviously been drinking before I had arrived and he was so incensed at the sight of my tattoo that he didn't hesitate to strike me. But this time I was quicker than him and ran straight into the kitchen. I saw a knife on the kitchen table, gleaming in the sunlight. Dad followed me into the kitchen and I grabbed the knife. I told him that if he ever touched me again I would kill him. He knew I meant what I said. He went back into the other room. I was shaking as I put down the knife. It worked though, because he never came near me again.

My plan was that Mum and I should go away together and completely distance ourselves from Dad. I reassured her that, together, we would have more strength and determination. I had reached the stage where he didn't frighten me any more, and I think Mum knew that, too. At last we made arrangements, with every detail carefully planned. I arranged to meet Mum the following Saturday morning at ten o'clock. I left early that morning and set off towards the High Street. More than likely Dad would still be in bed sleeping it off. As I stood waiting, I noticed the time on one of the shop's clocks. It was only 9.15 and I had hardly any money on me, about nine pounds.

It was snowing heavily and too cold to stand around for three-quarters of an hour, so I found a little coffee shop. I chose to sit at a table near the window and put my suitcase behind my chair. As I sat down, the owner brought over my hot cup of tea. I was more interested in holding the cup to keep my hands warm than drinking what was in it. As I gazed out of the window I wondered what the future held in store for Mum and me. I was scared she wouldn't come at first. Perhaps she was too frightened to come. What if Dad had seen her getting ready to leave and stopped her coming?

Perhaps he had given her a hiding into the bargain? There I sat watching the snow fall softly to the ground, covering the pavement like a white blanket. I glanced down at my shoes to find my feet were red raw from all the standing around outside, where the snow had seeped into the holes in my shoes. Before leaving the house that morning I had put some paper inside my shoes in the hope of covering up the holes, but now the paper was wet and soggy.

There were not many people in the coffee shop so I slowly took off one of my shoes and surreptitiously removed the paper, hoping no one would suspect anything. I screwed the paper up into a pulp and popped it into my handbag. I then did the same with the other shoe.

My table and chair were so positioned that I would be able to see when Mum arrived. I took another look at the clock and saw it was almost ten. I was beginning to feel uncomfortable and fidgety. I couldn't help thinking that neither Mum nor I had been very happy over the years, either when we were together or apart, but this time we really had to try to get away by ourselves.

I decided to get up and walk to the counter to order another cup of tea when I heard someone open the door of the coffee shop. I turned round and it was Mum.

'Get me one, love,' she said casually. She looked around the shop and then noticed my suitcase at the little table by the window, so she took another chair and placed it by the table. She put her suitcase next to mine and by the time she had settled herself I returned with the two teas. She picked up a newspaper which had been left on the chair before she came in, and opened it to the classified section to see what rooms were to let.

She looked at the date of the paper and said, 'This is last Wednesday's, but with a bit of luck not all the rooms will have gone. By the way, have you eaten yet, Ann?'

'No, Mum,' I answered.

Mum turned her head to look out of the window. The snow was getting worse. When she looked back at me she suggested we order something before we set off in that awful weather outside and, before I could answer, she had gone to the counter.

After we finished our meal Mum continued going through the newspaper, marking off suitable rooms to let. I sat quietly, admiring her face. Here she was, only thirty-eight years old and still attractive for her age with her slim build and now dark hair. She had not mentioned Dad at all and, although I was dying to ask her how she had managed to slip out without him knowing, I left it for her to tell me in her own time.

Just then, she looked up and smiled as if she knew all along what was going on in my head. 'Come on, cheer up, love. You'll see, it's all going to be all right.'

I smiled back at her and put my hand on top of hers. 'Oh, I'm OK, Mum. I just hope we can get somewhere to stay soon. I don't fancy walking around all day in this,' I explained.

'Come on then, love,' said Mum, reassuring me in her usual, familiar way. 'Let's get you some new shoes. I've got about forty or fifty pounds on me and if we go carefully with it I can afford to buy you a new pair.'

We left the warmth of the café and ventured out into the bleak, snowy weather. It was not letting up at all and it was bitterly cold. We went inside the first shoe shop we came across and I chose a suitable pair. We couldn't afford boots but what a difference new shoes made! At least my feet were dry now.

We spent all that afternoon telephoning people advertising rooms to let, and walking round to those with just addresses given to see if they had been taken or not. By four o'clock we had had no luck, so we made our weary way back to the High Street, from where we had started all those hours ago. We were both suffering from cold, and it was now starting to get dark.

'Let's go into Woolworths,' said Mum. 'At least we'll be a bit warmer inside.'

I was so cold by now I would have gladly gone in anywhere so long as I could get the feeling back into my fingers and toes. I felt sorry for Mum. I knew she was getting worried.

I put my arm around her shoulders and said, 'Don't worry, Mum. We'll manage to find somewhere to stay, some way or another.' 'I hope so, Ann,' she said and we picked up our two suitcases and walked around Woolworths for about half an hour.

When we came out of the store Mum suggested we try looking at the big houses in the opposite direction, just in case someone had put up a notice board advertising a room to let. So off we set towards the end of the High Street. As we walked past the huge clock tower there, Mum suddenly stopped in her tracks. She had caught sight of a notice board in the window of one of the large houses. I followed her pointed finger and sure enough, there, just past the clock tower, was a board in the window with 'ROOM TO LET' printed in large, bold letters. Thank God! I grabbed Mum's arm and, looking carefully to check there were no cars coming, we crossed the street. We pushed open the front gate and rushed up the path. Mum rang the doorbell and we waited for somebody to answer the door. It seemed like an age before an elderly lady opened the door and invited us in. We stepped into a warm and very large hallway. The room was still vacant, so after Mum and the lady agreed on the rent we followed her upstairs. We climbed up and up, three floors in all, and finally arrived at our room in the attic. The lady unlocked the door and showed us in. We put our suitcases down as we entered. It wasn't a palace, but we both gave a huge sigh of relief and shut the door behind us.

Chapter 4

It was quite a large room and as I looked around I saw a big double bed along one wall and in the middle of the room a small table with two chairs. In one corner stood an armchair and alongside that was a small sink. A kettle, some cutlery and crockery were on shelves above the draining-board and at the side of the sink, on the floor, was a small paraffin heater. There wasn't much in the room besides these things but everything was clean and tidy. Mum checked the paraffin heater whilst I put the suitcases on the bed. 'We're OK,' said Mum. 'There's enough paraffin in it for a couple of days.' She picked up the heater, placing it near the little table in the middle of the room and then she lit it.

'It shouldn't take long to warm the room up,' she said. She asked me if I was all right, at which I smiled and nodded. 'Well, it's not much, but I'm sure we'll be a lot happier here, don't you agree?' she said.

'Oh, yes, Mum, we'll be just fine,' and I gave her a big hug.

'Your clothes are soaking. Take them off before you catch your death of cold.'

'Yours are no better,' I said. 'The landlady said the bathroom was just along the hallway. I think I'll go and have a nice hot bath and then you can have yours.'

By the time I returned to our room Mum had unpacked and hung our clothes up. It was already beginning to feel like home. Mum had her bath and I had two mugs of soup ready. We had bought a few items of food in case we were lucky enough to find somewhere to stay.

I said, 'This'll warm us up,' and we sat on the chairs round the heater.

'I'll pop out to the shops in the morning and get some groceries,' said Mum, and started making out a list of the things we needed. 'We haven't much money, so we'll have to go carefully until we both get a job.'

'Don't worry, Mum. We'll start looking first thing Monday morning. I'm sure we'll be able to find some work without too much trouble.'

'I sincerely hope so. I've only been able to pay two weeks' rent in advance. Are you glad we're together, Ann?'

How could she ask such a thing? 'Oh, Mum, you don't know how much!' and I got out of my chair so I could hold her tight. After a few seconds Mum pulled back and looked at me squarely in the eyes.

'I'm so sorry, Ann, love.'

'Sorry? Whatever for?' I said, but of course I knew Mum was referring to all the times we had been apart from each other. I knew it wasn't Mum's fault. How could it be when I knew how much she loved me?

I said, 'Mum, I'm just glad we're together,' and gave her a kiss on the cheek.

Mum lit a cigarette but I noticed her hands were trembling a little.

'What's wrong, Mum? Are you worried in case Dad finds out where we're living?'

'Not really,' she replied. 'I'm still a bit cold from being out in that snow all day. Anyway, by the time your father came in last night I didn't get to sleep till the early hours, and even then I kept thinking about our running away today so that was on my mind and I didn't get much sleep.'

There was a small alarm clock near the sink. As I looked at it I could see it had gone past ten o'clock so I said, 'Come on, Mum. Let's get into bed. We'll be much warmer there and I think we're both tired out.'

Mum smiled and got up and got ready for bed.

As we lay there, we chatted for a while until finally Mum fell asleep. I felt much warmer now. I watched Mum for a while, pleased that we had managed to be together without worrying about Dad barging in in a drunken rage. The curtain at the window wasn't pulled properly so I could still see the snow falling outside. It felt good to be safe and warmly tucked up in bed. My eyes fell on my handbag, which was lying on top of my suitcase on the floor. It wasn't so much the handbag which occupied my mind as what was inside it. I had managed to buy enough pills to last me a couple of weeks, so at least I knew there was a sufficient supply and I didn't have to worry about buying any for a while. What I was worried about was how Mum would take it. I had never seen her take a pill for anything, not even a headache, and by God she must have had many of them in her time. I was confused because I was happy lying next to Mum, but concerned she was unaware of what I was doing to myself. I still had a great need for the pills and, although I had tried desperately to stop taking them a couple of times, I had found the after-effects too painful. As I looked at Mum, I wondered if there was any need to tell her yet. After all, we both had enough to worry about in the next few weeks, what with finding work and hoping Dad wouldn't find us. There was no point in adding to our problems by confessing I was taking pills. I decided that would be the best thing to do, turned over and very soon fell asleep.

We had a lovely long lie-in on the Sunday morning and spent the whole day relaxing. Apart from the fact we didn't want to do anything in particular, we couldn't go anywhere because of the bad weather and lack of funds, so we spent most of the time chatting. Mum was interested to know what I had been doing since we had last lived with each other. I told her most of it – except probably the most important part – the taking of drugs. I knew I would have no option but to tell her soon because living a lie was almost unbearable. I wouldn't be able to keep up the pretence for long and I was finding it difficult to find hiding places for my pills, let alone take them whilst living in one room together. However, that Sunday I left it, and made up my mind not to tell Mum, for we were so happy and I didn't want anything to spoil that contented feeling.

The following morning we left early in search of work. The first shop I tried showed interest. It was the little baker's shop not far from where we were living so I wouldn't have to worry about fares. The wages weren't much but enough to survive on till Mum could get a job, too. Mum didn't manage to find a job that day but mine started the following Monday. By the time Wednesday arrived we were gradually running out of money and Mum was worried.

She said, 'I'm afraid we'll have to live on bread and dripping until the money starts coming in, love.'

'Well, that'll be better than nothing,' I said. 'At least we've got a roof over our heads.'

Poor Mum looked so depressed I tried to cheer her up, 'I start work on Monday and you're sure to find a job before the weekend, you'll see. It won't be long before things improve.'

Sure enough, when we went out job-hunting on the Friday morning, Mum was given a job in a restaurant in North Harrow. The following week flew by and by Sunday we were both fed up with eating bread and dripping. We had it for breakfast, dinner and tea but we were very happy there all the same. We fully enjoyed the wonderful feeling of freedom to do exactly as we pleased without Dad spoiling it for us. It was a completely new way of life for us both. Mum would play a game and say, 'What would you like for dinner today, Ann?' and I would reply, 'Er, I think I'll have steak and chips today,' and Mum would put the bread and dripping in front of me and we would both roar with laughter.

I had only been at my job in the baker's shop for a few weeks when Mum came home one night to tell me there was a job vacant at the greengrocer's opposite the restaurant where she worked.

She said, 'If you apply for the job, Ann, at least we'll be working right near each other.'

Luckily I got the job and Mum and I left the flat together and even managed to get the same lunch hour and come home together in the evenings. We managed to build our little room into a small home and we were happier there than we had ever been before. It was spring and the snow had gone. I was still secretly taking the drugs; as far as I was aware, Mum had not found out or, if she had, she had not said anything. However, it was becoming increasingly difficult for me to hide them and there were so many times I wanted to talk to Mum about it, for I knew I was ill and there was nothing I could do about it on my own. I had found extra strength in the drugs and I didn't want to lose that feeling, no matter how happy I was with Mum.

I didn't realise how sick I was becoming. There were many times when I really didn't want the drugs to be such a major part of my life, but I didn't know how to survive without them. I decided that I would tell Mum all about it the following weekend. A couple of days before the weekend we were on our way home from work when Mum said, 'When we get in, love, I want a word with you.' I hadn't seen her so serious for a long time.

She opened her handbag and brought out an empty tube of the pills I was taking. For a moment I just looked at it. I had tried so hard hiding them the past few weeks and yet here she was holding one of them.

'Can I explain when we get in, Mum?' I asked in a croaky voice.

'OK, love,' said Mum, and nothing more was said on the way home.

When we got inside, Mum put the kettle on and took off her coat and shoes. She laid the table for tea whilst I got changed from my working clothes into a skirt and jumper. There was an awful silence, one of those moment when a sense of mistrust passes between two people. I think Mum was waiting for me to talk to her, but I was trying to avoid it, because I knew how much I had hurt her by keeping such an awful secret from her and she undoubtedly felt betrayed, a feeling which I would never knowingly bestow upon her, the one person in my life whom I loved so dearly.

Somehow or other we managed to finish our tea, but then Mum picked up her handbag again and brought out the empty tube.

'Ann, what exactly are they for and why are you taking them?' Mum asked.

'Mum,' I muttered apologetically.

'Hold it a minute,' said Mum. 'Before you tell me your story, I know what these pills are for. They're slimming pills and you can't be using them for that purpose because you are too skinny for starters. There's no reason you'd need anything like that, so I would like to know the truth.'

'OK, Mum,' I said, and I told her the whole story, right from the beginning. What I didn't tell her, however, was how many I was taking a day. My intake had gone up to fifteen or twenty a day but I told her it was only a few a day.

'What do you call a few, Ann?'

'Well,' I said, 'sometimes it's eight.' I tried my best to sound convincing and chose the number eight as a compromise. I knelt beside her and said softly, 'I can control them, Mum, honestly I can. They're not that bad, it's just that I need them for now.'

I went on to remind her of the past and how they had helped me cope with my difficulties.

'I promise that when we are settled I will stop taking them. It shouldn't be that difficult, honestly.'

I even got to believe the words myself. At sixteen I truly believed I was capable of anything. How wrong I was not only to deceive my mother, but myself also.

Mum cuddled me for a while and then said, 'I don't want anything else to happen to you, Ann, for you mean the world to me. We'll speak no more of it tonight, but I can't sit back and watch you kill yourself.'

I knew then she realised I was taking more than I had admitted to because, after I'd said I took no more than eight a day, she wouldn't have said such a thing. I just cuddled her and kept silent.

Life carried on and I had never enjoyed it so much. Both of us were much more relaxed and, although I was still taking the pills, neither of us talked about it, which suited me.

One day, during our lunch break, Mum pointed out a young man who was sitting near us at one of the other tables in the restaurant. He was one of the lads who worked at the radio shop, according to Mum. He was about thirty with fair hair. I wouldn't say he was terrific looking but he had a kind face.

He must have noticed me looking at him, for suddenly he looked at me. I quickly turned away to ask Mum what she had mentioned him for.

'Well,' she said, 'I thought I'd buy you a radio as there isn't one in our room and there's no television either, and I spoke to him yesterday about it. He told me to pop in and have a look at what they've got in the shop.'

'That's great. I'd love that,' I said. I looked at the clock in the restaurant. 'I've got to rush. See you at the bus-stop tonight, Mum.' I gave her a quick kiss on the cheek and went back to work.

That evening, Mum said, 'I tell you what, Ann, *you* go into the radio shop and choose which one you want. Go tomorrow if you like.'

I gladly accepted and thanked her. Having my very own radio! The following day I couldn't wait for my lunch-time to come then I went straight over to the radio shop. As I opened the door the young man was near the front of the shop.

'Can I help you?' he asked.

'Yes, please. My mother works next door and apparently she spoke to you about buying a radio and sent me in to choose one, because it's for me really.'

'Fine,' he said and smiled. 'Come in and I'll show you what we have.' His voice was soft and friendly and straight away I liked him. A young man in the back of the shop who was about nineteen said, 'Do you need any help, Tony?' and laughed cheekily at the fair-haired man. I laughed to myself for, without sounding big-headed, I was quite a nice-looking young girl and I suppose they were both trying to chat me up. I chose which radio I wanted and went in to tell Mum about it. I only had about ten minutes before I was due to go back to work, so I rushed in and said I had to go or I'd be late back to work. Mum said she'd leave work five minutes early and pop in and sign for it.

When I met Mum that night at the bus-stop she had the radio with her. I was so excited about it that as soon as we finished our evening meal and cleared away I put the radio on. Mum reminded me not to have it on too loud, in case it disturbed the people downstairs, but I'm sure she said it with a twinkle in her eye for she knew how much it meant to me.

As Mum stood ironing she said, 'I think that young man from the radio shop likes you.'

'Which one?' I replied, laughing and trying to show some modesty.

'The one who was sitting in the restaurant the other day. He asked me where you worked and if you had a boyfriend or not,' said Mum. 'But I think he's a bit old for you,' and looked that 'motherly-concern-for-her-only-daughter' type of look.

'Come on, Mum, he can only be in his late twenties. Anyway, there's no problem because I've only seen him twice so I shouldn't worry.' With that, I carried on listening to the music.

I noticed that during the next two weeks the fair-haired man happened to take his lunch hour at the same time each day as Mum and I. He sat at the next table to ours as before when we were eating our dinner. Very soon he was sitting at our table, and I found out that he was the supervisor of four shops, and on the day I had gone into the radio shop to choose my radio he had just happened to be visiting the shop himself. We soon became friends and I used to pop into the shop during my lunch hour instead of going into the restaurant. Mum didn't mind, quite happy to see me enjoying myself. The lads used to play cards in the radio shop so I started to join in with them. I now called the fair-haired man by his first name, and in a way wished he would ask me out. I could tell he was interested, but that was as far as it went.

One Sunday morning there was a knock at our door. Our landlady was standing there and told us there was a gentleman downstairs wishing to speak to me. At first Mum was alarmed and said, 'I'll be down in a minute. Can you tell him to wait a little while, please.'

Mum shut the door and started trembling. 'It's your father, I bet,' she said. 'It's all right,' I said, 'I'll go instead. If it is him he might think it's just me living here on my own. You never know, it might work.'

I knew Dad was only really interested in Mum, and if I

was to go to see him he might accept it and leave without any trouble.

'What if he's drunk?' Mum said with a sudden worried thought.

'I'll worry about that,' I replied, and before she could say any more I had gone. I had curlers in my hair and an old green coat draped over my shoulders. I could see the broad shoulders of a man through the window and I hesitated. With my hands shaking I managed to open the front door and there in front of me stood the fair-haired man, Tony.

'What do you want?' I blurted out rudely. I'd worked myself into a lather thinking it was Dad.

'Oh, I do apologise,' I said then. 'I thought you were someone else.'

His face seemed to drop so I went on, 'No, my father might have called by. I thought it was him.'

'Oh. I just wanted to return this to you,' he replied. In his hand he was carrying a playing card. It was the joker.

'You left it at the shop,' he added.

I thought to myself, What the hell is he on about? and then I suddenly remembered I had taken a pack of cards to play in the shop on Friday, but I must confess I couldn't remember leaving the joker card there or honestly caring whether I did or not. I didn't know whether to laugh or cry. Just before I had opened the door I'd been so frightened, and now here I was, standing in front of a man with a joker in his hand. 'Thanks!' I said. 'That was nice of you.' I thanked him once more as I took the card from his hand, and went to close the door, but before I could Tony blurted out, 'Would you like to go out tomorrow night?'

'Yes, that would be lovely,' I replied. 'I'd love to.'

He smiled and walked back down the path and as I watched him I thought to myself, Yes, I do like you, and with that I shut the door and went back upstairs.

'It's OK, Mum. We're safe. It was Tony.'

'Who's Tony?' asked Mum perplexed.

'You know, the guy from the radio shop. He wants to take me out tomorrow night,' I said.

'Are you going?' asked Mum.

'Yes I am. I rather like him. You don't mind, do you, Mum?'

'No, love,' said Mum with a smile. 'As long as you enjoy yourself, Ann, that's all that matters.'

From that time on Tony and I started to date regularly, and gradually we fell in love. I knew I would have to tell him about my illness one day but I was getting used to living day by day and, once again, I put it aside.

Mum and I decided to look for a bigger place to live. We found a flat in West Harrow owned by a lovely Irish couple who were kind to us. We enjoyed having more than one room to live in. We had now been together for about four months and life had a new meaning for us. Naturally, we were still worried about Dad ever finding us, but it didn't seem to matter so much for, as time went by, we learned how to live freely and got more used to his not being around.

One Friday night I had to work late so Mum went home well before me. I was going out with Tony later that evening. I looked at my watch as I walked up to the front door and was pleased to see I still had a couple of hours to get ready. I knew Mum would have my tea ready. As I walked up the stairs, unbuttoning my coat, I stopped half-way because I thought I could hear a man's voice. I froze. I couldn't mistake that voice – it belonged to Dad. I had to somehow put a brave face on and prepare myself to meet him, though I was still petrified of him. 'How on earth has he found us?' I knew I had no option but to go in and as I did I saw my father standing there as large as life as if nothing untoward had happened, and I could see that terrible look of fear in Mum's eyes again. I didn't know what to do. I tried to make polite small-talk, all the while sorting out in my mind the best course of action to take. In the end, I simply said in a calm voice, 'Oh, don't forget we have to go to the shops, Mum,' and by some unbelievable chance my father fell for the ruse. I can't really remember if he smelt of drink or not, but all he said was, 'All right, I'll wait here. You won't be long, will you?'

Mum and I said, 'No,' simultaneously and walked out of

the room shutting the door behind us. As soon as we were outside the house we ran with all our might. We kept on running until I felt physically sick. My first thought was where we could hide. As we passed an alleyway I grabbed Mum's arm and we ran a little way down it, then stopped, pressing our bodies up against the wall. It was dark, something in our favour. I don't know how long we had been sheltering there, it seemed like an eternity, when suddenly I saw my father's silhouette at the end of the alleyway, not facing our direction, but looking all around him. I turned my face to the brick wall, praying, not even daring to look at Mum, although I knew that she was pressed right up against the wall next to me.

After a while we heard my father's footsteps walking away but we continued to stay where we were, immobile, for a while longer, just to make absolutely certain that we were safe. After what seemed a lifetime we managed to return to the flat.

As soon as we got indoors Mum started to sob uncontrollably. I, too, was shaking, but I knelt down by Mum's chair and tried to console her.

'Come on, Mum,' I said softly, and I held her close. After a while she calmed down a bit and I made her a cup of tea.

'Wait there, Mum, I won't be long,' I said. 'I'm going down to have a word with the landlady,' and I slipped out of the door.

I went downstairs and knocked on their front room door. I told the couple all about my father and the predicament we were in. They were obviously concerned and sympathetic and after I had told them the whole story the husband said, 'Now don't you worry about a thing, love. Just tell your mother from me that there is no way your father will step over this threshold again.' I thanked him and bid them good night. It was very kind of him to say such a thing, but as I walked back upstairs I knew we would have to find somewhere else to live. Although they were a lovely couple they really didn't know how much trouble my father could cause. Before I could open the door to our room I heard a knock at the front door. My heart began to beat fast and I could feel horror overpowering me. I looked at the front door and could see the figure of a man standing there, knocking. I leant back and thought, Please don't bring trouble, Dad.

Mum opened the door to our room and came out to the top of the stairs to see what was going on.

'Sssh, someone's at the door,' I whispered, and saw Mum's face turn white.

We waited for our landlord to answer the door and a voice said, 'Hello, is Ann in, please?'

I sighed with relief. It was Tony! With all the trouble and comings and goings of the evening I had completely forgotten all about my date with him! The landlord had met Tony before so he shouted, 'Ann, your boyfriend's here for you,' and went back into his living room.

'Come up, Tony,' I shouted down and took Mum back into our room. I told Mum quickly what the landlord had said before Tony came in, because I hadn't told Tony about Dad before and what he was like. I loved Tony and thought he might well be put off seeing me any more if he knew what my father was like. But I had no choice now that Dad had found out where we were living, and I knew I had to tell Tony the truth. I didn't want to leave Mum on her own that evening, just in case Dad came back, so I just told Tony Mum wasn't well and could we make it the following evening?

That night I couldn't sleep, neither could Mum. I could hear her moving about and I knew she was worried about Dad coming back. I hated him so much. Why couldn't he leave us alone? Since I had been living with Mum, my pill intake had stayed at the same level. Although I couldn't stop taking them I was a lot happier and didn't need to increase the dosage. However, the happiness we had created over the past four months had been shattered and I was once again scared of what might be in store. For the first time in months I found myself turning to the drugs again for renewed strength. I was determined Dad would never get near Mum again and the pills would give me the courage and determination to stop him. I knew in my heart it wasn't really the answer, but for the time being it was the only answer I had. How on earth Dad had found our address I didn't know, but I did know that if he had managed to find that bit of information out then he would also find out where we both worked, and that worried me. We needed the money we earned to live on. And then there was Tony – I had to tell him, for knowing my father, he would no doubt find out about him, so I had to warn him to be on the safe side. I couldn't risk Dad hurting Tony. As I lay in my bed I thought about Tony more deeply. I had only known him a few months by now, but I had learnt that his background was completely different from mine. He was an only child and had had things fairly easy; how would he take learning about my Dad and the way he was? I hated Dad already, but if he did anything at all to spoil my relationship with Tony I would have hated him even more, if that was at all possible.

The next evening Tony and I dropped Mum off at her mother's house on our way out. We arranged a time to pick her up later that night and then Tony and I went off to a pub for a quiet drink. Tony soon sensed something was on my mind as we sat together in the cosy corner of our local, and asked me what the matter was. 'Nothing!' I said.

'Well, you're a little bit quiet tonight, Ann, and I want you to be able to share it with me. I might be able to help you, you never know,' Tony said, with a caring arm around my shoulder.

'We've had some problems at home, that's all,' I replied.

'Then don't you think you'd better tell me about them? I hate seeing you like this.'

For a moment I thought to myself, Should I just go ahead and tell him everything, including the drugs, or just about Dad? The chances were I might lose him one way or another anyway, so it was in for a penny and in for a pound. If I told him everything at least I wouldn't feel I had been cheating him or deceiving him.

I went into the whole background of my life: Dad's drinking and violence, my brother, Mum and the life we had led and, above all, about my drug addiction. I found it so much easier to tell Tony than I had ever imagined and felt like a great weight had been lifted from my shoulders. After I had finished telling him everything he was very quiet for a while. 'Well,' I asked, 'Aren't you going to say anything?'

'It makes no difference to me whatsoever about your father,' he said, 'but I am worried about your health. How many of these pills are you taking a day?'

'A couple,' I quickly retorted, lying through my back teeth. I went on. 'I can come off them whenever I want to. It's just that I need them for the time being to see me over this bad patch.'

'Are you sure?'

'Of course.'

Tony was still looking apprehensive and I felt there was something else he wanted to say. After a couple of minutes he said quietly, 'If it's a night for speaking the truth then I had better tell you my secret.' I was taken aback. What on earth had Tony got behind his back that I didn't know about?

He went on to say, 'I want you to know I really love you, Ann, no matter what, but . . . the fact is, I'm married!'

'Married!' I exclaimed, and sat there with my mouth open. Married? Impossible, I thought. There I was, worried sick about telling him about Dad and everything, but to me this was far worse. I had never asked him before if he was married or not because the thought never entered my head. When a guy asks a girl out for a date, and the relationship then blossoms and they fall in love, surely there's never a thought of whether he or she is already married.

'Let's go,' I said, getting up to leave. The tears were ready to flow and I wouldn't or couldn't cry in front of so many people. I walked out to the car with Tony behind me. He unlocked the car door and I got in. Everything was collapsing on top of me, my whole world was turned upside down and I burst into tears. The events of the previous evening, and now learning I was going out with a married man, were too much for me to bear. Tony sat there quietly until I gathered my senses. I wiped my tears away and turned to look at him.

'You'd better take me home,' I said, sobbing.

'Please don't be like that, Ann. My marriage is finished. I love only you.'

I didn't know whether to believe him or not and said to him again, 'Just take me home, please. I don't want to talk about it any more.'

'I don't want to finish it, Ann. I would have told you before but I was waiting for the right moment, and obviously this wasn't it. I'm so sorry,' Tony said, and with that put his key in the ignition and started the car up.

We picked Mum up from her mother's as arranged and I kept very quiet in the car all the way home. When we arrived Mum got out and went indoors.

'Ann, please don't finish it,' said Tony.

I loved him but I just couldn't think of anything but him having a wife. What chance did I have with my problems?

I said, 'No, it's better we finish it now because I just can't cope with all this at the moment.' I got out of the car and ran inside, shutting the front door behind me.

'What's the matter?' Mum asked, as she could see my eyes were red from crying.

I had to put on a show as she had enough on her plate.

I didn't tell her about his being married, just that we had had a row and split up.

'I like him, but that's all, so I've told him I don't want to see him any more.' I went on to ask how she was feeling and, although she said she was better now, she thought we should move on because Dad would keep coming round and we couldn't have that.

I said, 'We'll start looking for a new place next week, Mum. It shouldn't be too difficult to find somewhere suitable. I'm going to bed now. I'll see you in the morning.'

I gave her a good-night kiss on the cheek and went to bed. I couldn't get Tony out of my mind and kept thinking, Why me? I thought I had found myself a really nice man and he turns out to be married. That word, 'married', seemed to stick in my throat. I felt so mixed up. Would total happiness elude me for the rest of my life? I fell asleep telling myself not to wallow in self-pity.

During the next few weeks Tony was always on my mind but I saw nothing of him. I deliberately stayed away from the restaurant, making excuses to Mum that I was working for extra money during my lunch break. I knew I was very much in love with him and it hurt me so not to be with him any more, but it had to be that way as far as I was concerned. Once again, I turned to the pills and they helped me to cope.

One evening, Mum said to me, 'Ann, Tony came in to see me today at work.' My heart skipped a beat.

'Did he? What did he want?'

'He told me he was married,' she said, 'but it is you that he loves. He wanted me to have a word with you because he wants to see you so badly. I told him we were going to move soon due to your father and he offered to help us find somewhere to live. I really don't think you should get involved, though, Ann. He is married with children and I don't want to see you getting hurt.'

'I know he's married, Mum, and that's exactly why I've been avoiding him. The trouble is I do love and miss him so much. I don't know what to do and I must see him, Mum, I'm sorry.'

I promised to keep a level head though, and Mum said that was just as well, because Tony was going to pop in tomorrow lunchtime for my answer!

I said, 'OK, could you ask him to come round tomorrow night to see me, Mum, please?' I didn't want to break up his marriage and I was quite satisfied to just see him now and again. I could only really think of today and not the future, and to me a tiny amount of happiness was not too much to ask for at this stage in my life, surely. Tony came round the following evening, nice and early. I was still in the bath when he called, so Mum invited him in and whilst I was getting dried and dressed she had a chat with him. I was so pleased to see him, as I think he was to see me, judging by the look on his face.

Tony and I went out and as I got into the car he said, 'Thanks for coming. Where do you fancy going?'

'Let's go where we went last time,' I said, so off we went to the same little pub. There was very little or no conversation on our journey there. When we arrived we settled ourselves down at the same table as last time. When Tony returned with our drinks he asked me if I had heard any more from Dad, to which I replied, 'No, thank heavens.' I could sense Tony was nervous and trying his best to avoid the subject of his being married so I brought it up for him!

'Tony,' I said quietly, 'I've accepted you are married now and, although it still hurts, I am pleased we're together again. The main thing is, in no way do I want to be the cause of a broken marriage, but at the same time I am in love with you. So, if you want to see me now and again, I'll accept the situation for what it is.

You know I've many problems at the moment which I've got to sort out and I really can't take on any more, so if you do have a problem with your marriage, leave me out of it. I can't and won't take on your problems as well. I've given this matter a lot of thought and have come to the decision that if you still want to carry on seeing me we shall just enjoy what we have, and maybe we can keep what we have between us as it is.'

Tony spoke in a soft voice, 'But don't you want any more than that, Ann?'

'At the moment, no,' I replied quickly, and I really meant it. I finished my drink and Tony told me my Mum had had a word with him to make sure I wasn't hurt in all this, and he assured me he gave her his word. 'I wouldn't hurt you for the world, Ann, I mean it,' he said, and I believed him.

By the time we left to go home we were both a lot happier. It was now three weeks since Dad had come round to pay us a visit but we knew he'd be back so we managed to find a boarding house with a room to let and decided to move in there.

Chapter 5

We had only been living in the boarding house for about a month when the man who owned it asked Mum if she would like to manage it for him. Mum was delighted for it meant not only did we have a bedroom but also a sitting room with a small passage leading to a tiny kitchen. We both continued working and ran the house as well, which kept our minds occupied. There were four lads living at the boarding house, two of whom were male models, and we all got on fairly well. Once again, we forgot about Dad.

One Saturday I finished work early, which gave me a chance to do some shopping on my way home and still have enough time to get ready to go out with Tony. A couple of weeks previously he had mentioned his pending divorce. We had not brought up the subject again, and that was fine by me because I just wanted to forget it. I had had a successful afternoon shopping and was very cheerful as I got the bus home, looking forward to my evening out with Tony, but as I unlocked the front door I could hear Mum crying. I slammed the door shut behind me and rushed into the kitchen. The door was ajar and as I pushed it open there was Mum, sitting in the armchair. One of the young lads had his arms around her and she had what looked like a cloth in her hands, partly covering her face. I knelt down beside her and lifted her face. No one had to tell me what had happened to her nor who did it. I knew only too well. There was a large cut above Mum's eye which was bleeding badly, her eye was red and swollen and it was obvious she had been struck a blow by someone with a large fist. The young lad had tried his best at first aid by putting plasters across the cut, but it had only slowed the bleeding down very slightly. I hurried out to the first aid cabinet to fetch some more plasters while the lad kept hold of Mum, who was still trembling and sobbing. I took the cloth away from her, which I then realised was the kitchen tea-towel, and applied a clean face towel instead. I wiped the blood away as best as I could and put a larger plaster across the wound. The lad got up and went out, returning two minutes later with a large brandy.

'Give her that,' he said as he offered Mum the glass. 'It will help calm you down.'

'Thank you, love. You're very kind,' I said and held it for Mum to sip. I asked if Mum had told him what had happened and he said, 'No, she'd only been in a few minutes before you got here.'

'Are you feeling a little bit better now, Mum?' I asked. I was shaking myself but with anger, not pain, and if I had had any notion where that father of mine was at that precise moment I would have killed him without hesitation. After she had composed herself a little, Mum was ready to talk. 'I had gone out shopping in the High Street when suddenly he came out from nowhere. He grabbed my hair and punched me a couple of times in the face and then ran off, leaving me on the pavement.'

'Did anyone see what had happened or help you?'

'No,' she said. 'But, as I got myself up from the ground I noticed a car parked a little way up with a man sitting in the driving side. I ran up to him and asked him to take me home. He was very kind and wouldn't take any money. My head was hurting so badly I just wanted to get back here to safety,' then she started crying again.

'Come on, Mum,' I said, putting my arms around her. 'Let's get you into bed,' and with that I helped her undress. 'Try and get a bit of sleep, love. Nothing is going to happen to you now, so try to stop worrying.' I turned out the light and shut the door quietly behind me. I swore if it was the last thing I did, I would kill him.

I went back into the sitting room and swallowed a pill. Dad wasn't the sort of man to go quietly, he would always find some way of getting back. Making myself a cup of tea and lighting a cigarette, I sat down to gather my senses. I was determined he was not going to get the better of us.

43

I decided that when Mum got up I would discuss it with her. The last thing I wanted to do was to upset her, but I felt something had to be done about Dad. Tony came over before I woke Mum up and I told him all about what had happened. 'I know you told me about your father, Ann, but I never dreamt he was as bad as this. I really didn't realise he was that evil to do such a wicked thing to your mother. Why didn't she call the police?' he asked.

'I'm going to have a word with her when she gets up and see if I can persuade her to charge him with assault. I got her to rest for a little while because I thought it would do her good.' I paused a little, then said, 'Do you mind if we stay in tonight, I can't leave her in the state she's in and go out enjoying myself. I wouldn't be able to stop thinking about her, anyway.'

'No, love. Your mother comes first,' said Tony in his usual caring way. I made a fresh pot of tea and gave Tony a cup, then took one in to Mum. She was just lying there and I could tell she hadn't slept at all.

'Are you OK, Mum?' I asked.

'Yes, thanks, love,' she said. She sat up a little and asked if it was Tony I was speaking to in the sitting room.

'Come on, get up and come in with us, Mum,' I said, helping her to get steady on her feet.

As she came into the sitting room in front of me I could see Tony's face as he caught sight of her. For a split second he had a look of shock but quickly composed himself, and got up to help me guide her into the armchair.

'I think you should go to the police, Mum,' I said. 'If you don't he's going to think he can get away with it.'

'What's the point?' she said. 'I've called the police before about him but nothing came of it.'

'Well, maybe they couldn't do much then because you were living with him at the time, but surely now they can do something. Look, I'll tell you what I'll do,' and I turned to Tony and said, 'Tony, will you take me down to the police station?'

'Of course, if that's what you want to do.'

I knelt down by Mum and said, 'You stay right here, Mum. I'll have a word with the police and see what they can do. I won't be long.'

I got up, put on my coat and, giving her a peck on the cheek, told her not to worry.

When Tony and I arrived at the police station I pressed the bell for assistance and after only a few seconds a policeman appeared.

'Can I help you, miss?' he asked.

'Yes, please,' I replied. 'But is it possible to speak with someone privately in case someone comes in and hears what I have to say?'

He went to see if there was anyone I could speak to in confidence and asked us to take a seat. We waited for about ten minutes, at the end of which time a door to the side of the desk opened and out came a tall policeman. He asked us into his office, so I walked in and sat down. He shut the door behind him before he seated himself at the opposite side of his desk and asked what he could do for me. I told him the whole sequence of events. He listened intently to what I had to tell him and said, 'Well, I'm afraid there's not a lot I can do. Where does your father live?' I gave him the address and he assured me he would pay my father a visit to have a word with him, but he stressed that, unless they caught him actually hitting my mother, there was very little they could do. He went on, 'Unless your mother makes a charge against him and takes him to court, which I'm sorry to say most of the wives we see are too scared to do, our hands are tied.' I knew my mother would be too frightened of Dad to go to court.

The policeman went on to say, 'I'll tell you what, though, miss, always call us if he bothers you again.'

I got up and thanked him. Despite the fact I had not got anywhere, at least the policeman was kind and sympathetic, and not once did he give me the impression I was wasting his time.

Tony was sitting outside waiting patiently. 'Everything all right, love?'

I told him everything the policeman had said. 'That's a fat lot of good to us.' said Tony. He was a bit angry having seen Mum's badly beaten face, which was something he had never experienced before and it had had a marked effect on him. He added, 'I just hope one day he'll have a go at me and he'll find himself in court so fast, he won't know what's hit him.'

Tony suggested we get back to Mum to see if she was all right on her own. When we got back I told Mum all about my conversation with the policeman and I was pleased to see she looked a bit better than when we had left her.

Our landlord seemed to be happy with the way Mum had been running the house and we very rarely saw him. For the next six months things went fine. We had settled down again and life was improving. Mum and Tony had not mentioned the pills, but I was still taking them. At least my daily intake had not increased for some time, and they continued to make me feel I could keep my head above water. Tony and I were seeing each other regularly. He still lived under the same roof as his wife and their children, but he had decided to separate from her.

Tony's mother ran the RSPCA centre in Hillingdon and one day I asked Tony if he could get a dog for me. I had already asked Mum if she minded and she said it would be a good idea. So, one evening, Tony turned up with a young bitch. She was only about a year old and her owners didn't want her any more. As soon as I saw her little face I fell in love with her. She was only a mongrel, but to me she was the most beautiful dog I had ever seen. All through my childhood I had never been allowed to have any pets and had always wanted a dog of my own, and now here she was. I called her Sally and everywhere I went she came with me. Mum even allowed Sally to sleep at the side of my bed at night.

One evening, Mum and I were sitting in the back sitting room. Mum had just made us a cup of tea and brought it in from the kitchen. We sat chatting when, suddenly, Sally got up and went to the back door. I followed her, wondering if she wanted to got out to the garden, but then she started barking.

46

'Shut up, Sally,' I shouted.

'What's the matter with her?' Mum called.

'I don't know. Just ignore her,' I said, and went back to my armchair and cup of tea.

Sally carried on barking so I had to get up again to see what was wrong. It was out of character for Sally to continue barking so long. I put my cup on the table and walked over to the back door where Sally was. I bent down and patted her on the head and said, 'For goodness sake, Sally. What's all the commotion about?' and I went closer to the door. We didn't have a curtain up so I could see right out to the garden. I looked down at the lock and as I unlocked it I was startled to find there was a man crouching down outside. It was Dad, and I jumped back, and fell over Sally.

'Mum, quickly, get David!' I called to Mum. David was one of the young lads staying at the house at the time. 'Dad's outside!' I picked myself up from the floor. We both rushed towards the sitting room door, thinking he would try to get in by the back door. We stood in the hallway and by that time David was rushing down the stairs saying, 'What the hell's going on?'

I explained and went through the sitting room and into the kitchen, leaving Mum and me in the hall. Sally was still barking like mad and I feared for her safety.

Five minutes later David returned. 'It's OK,' he said. 'He's gone. If he comes back give me a call and I'll sort him out.'

He gave Mum a big hug, 'Come on. He won't try anything with people in the house, surely?' Mum just smiled.

Very cautiously, we walked back into the sitting room and I checked the kitchen door to make sure it was locked. Sally had calmed down now and, although I still felt uneasy, I was relieved he had gone and that there was someone else in the house and that we had a dog to protect us.

The following night when Tony came round I told him what had happened 'Mum didn't seem too bad today, considering, but he's found out where we live, and I know he'll be back.'

I was far more frightened than I let on to Mum and Tony and, instead of showing it, I took a couple of extra pills to make me feel better. At least they helped take the edge off for the time being. Now Dad knew our address he could be back any time and that was an awful thing to know. Mum and I had to be on our guard at all times. It was good that we worked opposite each other because it meant we left home in the mornings together and most evenings we came home together. The only thing was, I didn't want to go out in the evenings and leave Mum on her own. It was all right if one of the lodgers was in but even then I didn't feel settled in my mind. I was fortunate because Tony understood my predicament completely and agreed we should stay in every night in the weeks that followed. But the waiting was wearing me down.

My intake of pills increased dramatically. Tony said, 'Look, it's no use worrying to the extent that it makes you ill, Ann. If and when your father comes round, all we have to do is to call the police and they will deal with him. You are worrying yourself silly before anything has happened.'

I never intended to involve Tony much in our problems, but I was glad he wanted to be and I thanked him for being so wonderful about the whole thing.

'Ann, I love you, and your problems are mine as well, it's as simple as that,' he said.

It was time for him to go home so I got his jacket and walked to the front door with him. We stopped in the hallway and Tony held me close. 'Come on, love,' he said softly. 'I doubt very much if your father will come back here again, so stop worrying, OK?'

He had his back to the front door so that meant I was facing it. There was a small pane of glass at the side of the door and, and as Tony kissed me good night, there was an almighty crash. I looked up and saw a hand come straight through the glass! Tony immediately jumped out of the way and, as I stood there in wonderment, I watched the hand vanish. For a few seconds I was too shocked to move. The only thought I had was, 'You bastard, why can't you just leave us alone!'

Mum rushed out and held me because I was shaking like a jelly and crying.

I said I was all right but as I looked at her I felt that, for the first time since she and I had been living on our own together, I wasn't the strong one any more and I was glad to have Mum's arms around me.

After smashing the glass Dad had run off somewhere. My father was an extremely strong man and so no one in their right mind would take him on, but, he was scared of the police and he must have known we would call them. We weren't on the telephone so Tony went out and rang the police from a callbox and Mum and I tried to compose ourselves, sitting down in the sitting room.

The police came but told us that there wasn't much they could do except keep an eye on the house and that they would pay him a visit. It was the same old story – unless they caught him in the act there was very little they could do. Tony stayed after the police went, but I told him he had better go home because I knew he had to be up early next morning and it was now very late.

'Only if you're sure you will be all right,' said Tony.

'Yes, love, you go, and thanks for staying with us,' I said and I saw him to the front door, where we said good night.

When I returned to the sitting room I gave Mum a kiss and told her I was going to go to bed, if she didn't mind. Mum said she had calmed down a bit by now and asked me if I was all right. I sat back down beside her. I could sense she was worried sick about me and I didn't want that. So I just smiled and said, 'I'm fine Mum. Dad will soon get fed up with coming round here, you mark my words,' and after feeling I had convinced her, I went off to bed.

As I lay in bed I knew I was kidding myself about Dad. There was no way he'd give up. I felt exhausted, even the extra strength the pills had provided me with had disappeared. I started to cry as everything crowded in on me. Why us? I kept asking myself. I was worried about my increasing addiction to the pills, but without them I felt I couldn't fight Dad and I was well aware they were making me feel ill all the time. I tried not to let outsiders see but I knew in my heart what they must be doing to me. I felt remorse for all the lies I had told Mum and Tony about the amount of pills I was taking daily and I desperately wanted to tell them the truth. I couldn't though, because I knew they would nag me to come off them, and I just couldn't cope with that and the threat of Dad returning at the moment. I was so hooked on the pills by now that I felt my life depended on them. I realised that if I had been happy I would never have had to take the damn things in the first place. I lay for hours that night going over everything in my mind.

In the next few weeks Dad came round to the house on a regular basis, always drunk and argumentative. We couldn't inform the police because as quickly as he appeared he went away again.

One day, David, one of our lodgers, came up with an idea to try and help us put a stop to Dad coming round any more. My father always came through the back garden now and David decided to wire the garden in zig-zag fashion, so that father would trip over one of them and it would act as a form of warning system to us. If it worked, and he fell, he would surely make a noise and we would be bound to hear him. So, the following evening, David rigged up his invention and when he had completed his work in the garden he came indoors.

He said to Mum, 'Now, just in case he's clever enough to miss them all, which I very much doubt because it's getting dark now, I'll take a bucket of water up to my room and if he makes for the back door I'll get him with it.' We thought it was an ingenious idea. His bedroom was at the back of the house so he had a clear view of the back garden. He invited us up to see what would happen if Dad came round that evening so we eagerly followed him upstairs and sat down to wait. Very soon I caught sight of Dad at the bottom of the garden. Whenever I saw my father I felt intimidated and it was no different that night, even though it appeared that we had upper hand. In a way I felt ashamed and embarrassed because whenever Dad had caused trouble before we had been on our own, but now David was watching and that made a lot of difference. I was totally amazed for, somehow or another, Dad managed to step over each and every trip wire. By the time he reached the back door, and was standing immediately below David's bedroom window, he had missed every single wire! David couldn't believe his eyes either. He looked at Mum and said, 'Did you see that?' He held the bucket of water out of the open window, intending it to go all over Dad's head, but to everyone's astonishment it missed him completely. It was as if Dad was so drunk he didn't realise what was happening. He turned round to face the back of the garden and staggered back down it, once again missing all the wires. It was unbelievable, but deep down I was glad it was over. It was somewhat out of character for Dad just to walk away and I feared retaliation. It was also that to see him make a fool of himself as he had done in front of somebody he didn't know, hurt me, and from that day on I vowed I would never involve anyone else. If anyone was to fight Dad it would be me, only me.

Chapter 6

After that night, Dad kept right away from us. I still had that underlying fear that some day he would turn up out of the blue, but it was a good few months before he showed his face again. We were beginning to all feel more settled in our lives, but I still relied upon drugs. One Saturday after I had finished work I went to the chemist's to collect my pills. I looked towards the shelf where they were always on display for sale but, to my horror, they had gone. I tried to console myself by telling myself they must have had a change around in the shop and they had put them somewhere else.

I walked up to the counter and said to the assistant, 'Excuse me, please. Could you tell me where my pills are? I don't see them in their usual place.'

She said, 'Oh, they've been put on prescription now. You'll have to get them through your doctor from now on.'

I tried to look calm and thanked her, but inside I was going to pieces. As I walked out of the chemist's I was in a state of shock. What on earth was I going to do now? There was no way I could manage without them and the only way I'd be able to keep *taking* them was to get them with a prescription. All the way home that evening I was in a whirl. By the time I got home I didn't feel at all well and felt like going straight to bed. Mum asked me what the matter was but I bluffed my way out of it by saying I thought I had a cold coming.

'What shall I tell Tony when he comes?'

'Don't worry, Mum. He said he wouldn't be around till later tonight so I'll see him then. I just want a little lie down,' and with that I went to bed.

I knew there was very little choice but to accept the situation. The pills were now off the market and I wished I was dead, I knew there was no way I would be able to cope and tried to be rational about it, but it appeared that everything was against me. At that moment I hated the world and God.

Since we had moved to the boarding house I had kept notes in a diary.

It helped me to write down my thoughts, when I couldn't talk things over with Mum or Tony, because it was easy for me to express my inner feelings by putting them all down on paper. My diary was very private and personal to me and, in a way, a life-saver. Instead of bottling everything up I wrote everything down in it, putting it back in a secret hiding place so nobody but I would know it existed.

As I lay on my bed I picked up my little diary and started to read it. I flicked the pages until I came across the part where I had written how much I hated the pills, and that was exactly how I was feeling right now. I bent down to pick up my handbag from the floor and took out a tube of pills. I always had a week's supply in hand and I sat up to count them out. I had just about enough to last me until the following Tuesday. What on earth was I going to do when they had all gone? I started to shake and burst into tears. I couldn't go to Mum for help. I wondered if Tony would be able to help me. No, he hated the pills too, just as much as Mum did, so it would be no use telling him.

Mum walked in. 'Tony's here, love,' she said. 'Are you sure you're well enough to go out?'

I was a bit flustered, and as I answered Mum I tried to look busy so she wouldn't suspect I had the pills on my bed and my secret diary. I asked her to tell Tony I would be out soon. I rushed round putting my things straight and made myself presentable.

When I came in from seeing Tony later that night, Mum was already in bed asleep. Sally was sitting at the door waiting for me to come home. She was always pleased when anyone came in and wagged her tail happily. The problem with the pills was still very much on my mind. After I had said good night to Tony and he left to go home I decided to take Sally for a walk. Maybe I'd be able to come up with the answer as I walked with her. Perhaps I'd be able to see the situation in a different light and come up with a solution. I checked that my front door key was safely in my pocket and Sally and I set off, shutting the door quietly behind us. It was well past midnight and the streets were empty. Normally I liked the peace of the night, but I couldn't feel serenity this night. Surely, there must be somebody who could help me? I thought.

Just then Sally started tugging at her lead. I stopped to let her spend a penny and as I waited I looked all around. It was a clear night and the moon made everything bright and shiny. After a couple of minutes Sally was ready to continue our walk and, as I turned to pull Sally to come with me, I noticed a board which was mounted upon the garden gate near where we had stopped. I had never noticed this board before and was curious to see what it said. I went closer and saw that it had the word 'Doctor' printed on it and underneath the doctor's name were the times of his surgery hours. I looked up at the front door and noticed a small box alongside it. Printed on the outside of the box was the word 'prescriptions'. My imagination was working overtime. I wondered if, by any chance, there would be somebody taking the same pills as me and had a prescription made out for them ready for collection. I started to tremble at the mere idea. I knew what I wanted to do, but had never done anything like this before.

All of a sudden, Sally started barking, which made me jump. I pulled on her lead and patted her on the head.

'Ssh, Sally,' I whispered, and looked once again at the box. I plucked up enough courage to open the lid of the box, took out all the prescriptions and stuffed them quickly into my pocket. I walked back home as fast as my legs would go, dragging poor Sally behind me. I wasn't sure if anyone had seen what I had done, and I knew if I was found out I'd be in trouble. When I arrived home I shut the front door behind me and gave a sigh of relief. I got undressed as quickly as I could, got into bed, then laid out all the prescriptions on top of the bedclothes. I read each one in the hope that one of them would be for the drugs I was taking. To my dismay there was nothing at all of interest to me. I flopped back on my pillow. I was very disappointed that I didn't find what I was looking for. *Now* what do I do? I thought. I was getting tired now, so I put the prescriptions away in my handbag and settled down to sleep.

When I woke up the following morning stark reality hit me. I felt sick, a nervous wreck. I had got myself into this mess and somehow or another I had to get myself out of it.

That day Mum and Tony must have noticed my dreadful behaviour but, thankfully, didn't question me. The stolen prescriptions remained in my handbag until the Sunday evening when I went to bed. I took them out to examine them closely. I had only two days to go before my pills ran out and, as I looked at the prescriptions in front of me, I thought they were my last hope, but how exactly I wasn't quite sure. There must be something I could do with them to get me my drugs. It is amazing how strong willed a person can become when they want or need something that badly, and I was getting desperate. The idea came to me when I noticed a big gap below an item on one of the prescriptions. If I was extremely careful I might be able to write down the name of my drug in that gap and if I could copy the style of handwriting of the doctor who had made it out, nobody would be the wiser.

I rushed to find a pen and a piece of paper and started to copy the doctor's handwriting over and over again until I was satisfied that it was virtually the same. I sat up until the early hours and when I was ready I copied the writing on to the prescription. It looked just as if the doctor had written it himself and I was very impressed with my efforts. The biggest challenge was yet to come, of course, and that was when I took the prescription to the chemist to be made up. Would he or she be able to tell if I had forged part of it, or would it be good enough to go unnoticed?

I left for work early on the Monday morning, making an excuse to Mum that I had been asked to do some overtime. I hated lying to her and of course what I intended doing now was far worse, but I had got this far and there was no turning back. I was frightened and ill with worry, but it was my only hope. I got to the chemist's before it opened. I might be a little late getting to work so I had an excuse ready just in case. As I waited for the shop to open my heart felt as if it was in my mouth. My head was thumping as I feared the chemist would notice the prescription I was about to hand over had been tampered with. I was sweating as I paced outside the shop. After a couple of minutes I heard the key turn in the lock and then the bolts undone.

'Good morning!' said the man, smiling.

'Good morning,' I replied in a shaky voice. 'Er, can I give you this?' and I passed the prescription to him. He looked at it.

That's it, Ann, I thought to myself. You're in trouble now, he's looking at it too long. He knows there's something wrong with it, I convinced myself. I wanted to run but my legs just didn't want to move.

The chemist smiled at me and said, 'If you'd like to wait for ten minutes I'll do it for you now.'

'Couldn't you make it five?' I said, and walked out of the shop. I had to because I was shaking. I thought to myself, that was a stupid thing to do, he's bound to wonder what on earth is wrong with me. I stood still once I got outside the shop and gave myself a good talking to. 'Compose yourself, Ann, for goodness sake,' I heard myself saying. I managed to calm myself and walked back into the shop. To my relief the chemist didn't appear to have noticed my peculiar behaviour and told me my prescription was ready.

I thanked him and, with the pills in my hand, walked out and went to work.

From then on it became easy, perhaps too easy, to repeat the procedure. Naturally, I never let on to Mum or Tony what I was doing and, as we hadn't heard from Dad for some time, as far as they were concerned, things were looking up. If only they knew!

I continued to take a handful of prescriptions from the box as I had done the first time but after a few weeks I was finding it more difficult. The whole situation was making me feel ill, and there were times when I even wanted to be caught. It would have to be something like that to make me stop. My wish was soon granted, for one day, whilst I was at work, I had a visit from the police. I was asked to go down to the police station, where the Detective Sergeant wanted to have a word with me. I was expecting something like this to happen, but also glad they had gone to my place of work and not to my home, so at least I was able to keep it from Mum and Tony. My boss asked me what was going on and I told him it was about an accident I had witnessed.

I was so terrified about going to the police on my own that I made up my mind to tell Mum and Tony all about it before I went. So, after work that evening, I put Mum in the picture and told her everything. She was terrific and did her best to calm me down before Tony arrived. He, too, showed such strength and support and they both came with me to the police station. I had been given the name of the Detective Sergeant whom I was to ask to ask for and was shown into his office. Mum and Tony waited outside for me. A gentleman in his forties at a desk saw me enter the room, and got up inviting me to take a seat.

'Hello, you're Miss Pinkham, I understand,' he said. He obviously sensed my awkwardness and embarrassment. He went on, 'It's all right. I'm not going to bite your head off!' He had a kind face and smiled. 'But I must ask you a few questions, and I must ask you to be honest with me because I want to help you. If you don't tell me the truth I can't assist you.'

I still wasn't quite sure why he wanted to see me. I had an idea it was concerning the prescriptions, but I wasn't going to mention them unless he asked me out-right. His hand went down to the drawer in his desk and he brought out a handful of prescriptions and put them in front of him. I thought to myself, I knew it! and was glad I had come clean by telling Mum and Tony beforehand.

'Did you write on the prescriptions?' the Detective Sergeant asked me.

'Yes,' I replied, bowing my head.

57

There was no point in denying it and he seemed such a pleasant man.

He asked me why I had done such a thing and I told him the whole story. All the time he sat quietly, listening and waiting for me to finish. He didn't interrupt and, because he came across as a friendly, caring man, I found it easy to talk to him.

As I came to the end of my tale he picked up the prescriptions and flicked through them.

I concluded by saying, 'I can't lie any more. I just can't live without the drugs, and without some form of help I feel I'll have to carry on stealing the prescriptions. I'm sorry, but that's how dependent I am upon them.'

He looked up at me in astonishment. 'Are you being completely honest? You know it's a crime to forge and steal, don't you?'

I nodded, feeling ashamed on one hand and bitterly sad on the other.

'Yes, I know it's wrong and I realise the trouble I'm in, but that's how it is.'

He got up from his chair and rubbed his chin with his hand.

'Look,' he said, 'Will you pop in here at the same time tomorrow? In the meantime I'll see if I can get you some help. I can't promise you but I'll try.'

I shook his hand and thanked him. As I came out of his office, Mum and Tony stood up, looking worried sick about me.

'Come on,' I said, 'I'll tell you all about it in the car going home,' and I could see the relief on their faces.

The following evening, instead of going to see the kindly Detective Sergeant at the police station, he came to me at home. He told me he had found someone who would help me and made me promise not to forge any more prescriptions. With the knowledge that someone would try to sort out my problems, I promised. I felt as if a great burden had been lifted from my shoulders. Hopefully, in the next few days, someone would come to see me and it would be all right.

After the Detective Sergeant left, I knew it would be hard to keep my word. I had tried before and hadn't succeeded, but that had only been for a day and I could vividly remember the pain then. I only hoped he could find help for me soon. I had only enough pills for one more day and I was glad that the day after would be the weekend, which meant I wouldn't have to go to work. I used to work most Saturdays but this Saturday was my day off.

All day Friday I tried to put it behind me and Mum and Tony both promised to help me as much as possible. On Friday evening when Tony was taking me home, just before he left me, he said that he would be round the following morning. Both he and Mum knew more than likely I would not be well, but exactly how unwell no one could foresee. When I woke up I didn't feel too bad but by lunchtime I had started vomiting. I kept being sick right up until the late afternoon, by which time I couldn't stop shaking either. Mum insisted I go to bed as I was in a terrible state. Tony hadn't arrived yet, I don't know what had held him up, but in a way I was pleased he wasn't around as I felt so ill and really didn't want to see anyone, just to curl up in bed. Tony finally arrived early evening and Mum explained to him how I had been all day.

'Sorry I'm late, love,' he said to me, as he popped his head round my bedroom door. 'How are you feeling?'

I burst into tears. I couldn't talk to him as I felt so awful.

With that, Tony came right into my room and sat on my bed, holding my hand.

'I can't stand the pain any longer,' I sobbed.

'Come on, you can make it,' Tony said reassuringly and he put his arms around me. 'I'll stay the night with you.'

'But won't it create problems for you at home?' I had to ask.

He replied, 'No, it'll be OK, don't worry.'

I didn't get a wink of sleep that night. My whole body was racked with pain. I had taken the last pill on Friday evening at 6 p.m. and by Sunday morning I would have given anything to have another pill. Tony and Mum both knew this, and Mum had cried during the night as she held me close to her, cradling me in her arms. She just couldn't sit there and bear to see me in so much agony. As she held me she said softly, 'If professional help doesn't come soon for you then . . .'

Mum didn't finish her sentence but stopped. She just held me closer and Tony sat the other side of me.

By the time the morning came the sickness was not so bad but my body was still hurting. As I lay in my bed all I kept asking was, Why me? Why me? I didn't ask for the pills and I didn't ask for the pain I was suffering. The tears rolled down my face and I could hardly move. Mum and Tony had had no sleep either but, nevertheless, Mum got up and made me a slice of toast and tea.

'Come on, love, it will settle your stomach and maybe ease the sickness,' Mum said softly.

I took Mum's advice as I could see they were both worried about me. After I had finished the tea and toast Mum suggested I try to get some sleep and beckoned to Tony to follow her out of the room.

I could hear them talking in the other room as I lay there, but my head was hurting too much to concentrate on what they were saying. Despite the fact that they were speaking quietly it sounded loud to me, so I put the pillow over my head to blot out the noise a little. I kept thinking of the Detective Sergeant to whom I had given my word and whom I didn't want to let down, but on the other hand I couldn't keep up with the pain. It was getting too much to bear, and I knew what I had to do.

I got out of bed quietly, having remembered that there were some old prescriptions hidden at the back of one of the drawers in my dressing table. My hands were shaking as I held them, for I knew it was wrong, but I also considered it wrong for me to be put through so much pain and agony. I put the prescriptions in my handbag. I crawled back into bed, knowing I couldn't get any of the prescriptions made up until Monday. I just hoped I could hold out until then and manage to change one at the chemist's without anyone realising how ill I was. It was only the fact of knowing I was going to get the pills the following morning that got me through that Sunday. Mum had already told my place of work I wouldn't be in till the middle of the week. Tony stayed with me till late Sunday evening and Mum had managed to get a couple of hours' sleep herself, but by that time my bottle had gone. I sat on the settee shaking all over and, as I looked at them, I told Mum and Tony, 'It's no use. I can't do it. I can't go through another day without them. It's no use arguing with me, I am not going to have this pain any longer!' And I went on and on about it.

Mum got up from her chair and came over to me, putting her arms around me. She looked over at Tony and said to him, 'There must be something someone can do for her. I can't see her suffering like this.'

Tony got up and knelt down beside me, holding my hands, which were trembling more than ever.

He suggested that he go to a doctor the next day as things were getting out of hand. By this time my body was jerking in the most violent way and the pain was intense. I couldn't bear it any longer, it was hurting too much. I kept muttering, 'No more, no more.'

'Come on, love,' said Mum, 'let's get you back to bed.'

It was getting late, so Tony came into my room and said he would be back in the morning as soon as he could make it.

'No,' I said. 'Make it the afternoon.'

Although I had told them I couldn't take any more I hadn't told them what my dishonourable intentions were regarding the prescriptions in my handbag. I decided it would be best to tell them afterwards, for I knew if I were to tell them now they would stop me.

I thought the following morning would never come. I watched the clock every hour until daylight. Mum was very reluctant to go to work, but I persuaded her I would be all right on my own. After a lot of convincing she got herself ready and when I heard her slam the front door behind her I dragged myself out of bed. I took a look at myself in the mirror and had a fright. I looked absolutely terrible. My hands were still shaking as I tried to put a bit of make-up on, but I managed it somehow. Slowly I got dressed and finally was ready to put my plan into action. I looked up at the kitchen clock. It had just gone nine o'clock, so that meant the chemist's would be open for business.

As I walked down the road all the promises I had made to everybody, including myself, had gone out of the window. All I could think of was taking those damned pills, and that by lunchtime I would no longer be in this wretched pain.

The thought of being in trouble with the law didn't concern me, only getting rid of the pain I was in. I was given the pills without any bother and went straight back home with them.

Almost straight away I felt much better. I carried on that way for a couple of months until I had used up the last of my secret supply of prescriptions. Not once did I consider contacting the Detective Sergeant to tell him no one had been round to see me. It may have been that I thought he didn't care after all, though I know now that I was wrong to take that attitude.

It wasn't long before I was to meet him again, however, for one day when I went into a different chemist's with a prescription I felt a hand on my shoulder. I turned round and, to my horror, saw it was him.

'You had better come along with us, Ann,' he said quietly, and I had no choice but to leave with him and his constable. They drove me to the police station and ushered me into the same office I had been in before. They told me to sit down and left no doubt in my mind that this time they meant business. I was filled with remorse and self-pity.

As the Detective Sergeant sat down at his desk he told me he had sent someone to fetch my mother.

'I'm sorry, Ann, but this time I have got to charge you,' he said. I could tell he really was sorry by the tone in his voice, and that made me feel a little better. He asked me why on earth I had carried on stealing and forging since our last meeting and I explained that not a soul had come

62

to see me. His face dropped in disbelief and I could tell he was angry.

'I'm sorry, Ann. I didn't know, but they'll get a rocket from me, mark my words. This makes me feel worse for charging you, but it's my job and I have to abide by the rules.' He showed such compassion.

'What will happen to me now?' I asked.

'Well, you'll have to go to court first of all and it will be up to the magistrate to decide what punishment you deserve. I'm afraid you'll have to stay here tonight.'

This part shook me.

'Come on, you'll be all right,' he said, trying to calm me down.

There was a knock on the door and a policeman walked in. 'Her mother's here, sir,' he said.

'Thanks,' the Detective Sergeant said. He told me he would give me ten minutes with my mother and that was all he could allow us. He added that Mum had been told exactly what was going on and why I was there, and with that he left the room. A few seconds later Mum entered the room and held me close. She said, 'It's not fair, it's not fair. You've never done anyone any harm.' She held me at arm's length and looked at me. 'Don't worry, love, I'll get you a good solicitor. You are a sick girl and they will see that for themselves, so nothing will happen to you, I promise.'

Those ten minutes went far too quickly and soon it was time for Mum to leave. I asked her to tell Tony and kissed her goodbye.

When I was taken to court the following morning Tony was already there with Mum at his side. I wasn't permitted to speak to them but Tony smiled and gave me the thumbs-up sign. I felt a little better knowing they were both present to give their support. As I stood in front of the magistrate the Detective Sergeant stood up and read out the charge sheet. He then went on to explain how I had got into such a mess and how nobody had been to assist me with professional advice. The magistrate listened very carefully and, when all the evidence had been given, said, 'It is a very serious offence.' He said that he could understand the reasons why I had done it, but I would have to go to Holloway Prison for one week to have medical reports made out. As I looked towards Mum and Tony tears rolled down my face. I was so frightened.

Once I arrived at the prison, everyone was very kind. I got on well with the other girls. I had to see a doctor from a special hospital. When, at the end of the week, I returned to court, her report was read out by the magistrate. Then she looked up at me and told me I was to go to a hospital in in Shenley. She went on to warn me that if, for any reason, I should appear before her again, I should expect a stiffer sentence. I met Mum and Tony in the hall outside the courtroom and they both hugged me. 'I've got your clothes in the car,' Mum said and tried to give me a little smile. 'They said you have got to go straight to the hospital,' she said, still hugging me.

We came out of the courts, holding hands, and as we walked along the street we heard a loud shout. In absolute horror I turned round and saw my father trying to cross the road. He was waving his arms about, trying to attract our attention. How the hell did he know where to find us? I wondered. Apparently, my photograph had been in the papers and he had read all about me.

Tony grabbed my arm and said, 'Quickly, this way,' and, with Mum in tow, we managed to get into the car and away before Dad could catch up with us.

I was shaking like a leaf with fright. Tony tried his hardest to console me. 'He can't get you now, Ann, you'll be out of the way for a little while, somewhere he won't be able to find you.'

Yes, but for how long? I asked myself. I tried to calm down by reminding myself that I was free and that I wasn't going to allow my father to spoil our day. We had a few hours before we reached the hospital to enable us to unwind and put things into perspective.

Whilst I stayed in hospital I had the best treatment available, and they managed to cure me by gradually reducing my intake of the drug I was addicted to until I was on none at all. For the first two months everything went well. I saw Tony every day and at weekends I used to go home to see Mum. There had been no word from Dad since that day outside the court and I wasn't so worried about Mum's safety because Tony used to pop in to see her during the week. Apart from that, Mum had the lodgers living there, and there wouldn't be much Dad could do to her with them around.

One day the doctor came to see me whilst I was in hospital. I had been there about two and a half months and was beginning to feel much better.

The doctor said, 'Ann, your father is in my office and would very much like to see you.'

I swallowed hard and all the old feelings came charging into my body once more. It was too early in the day for Tony to come to visit me and without him I knew I was completely on my own. I said to the doctor, 'I don't want to see him, I'm too frightened.'

The doctor knew full well what my reaction would be but he had to tell me all the same. He said he would tell Dad what I had said, but added that he couldn't stop him from coming to the hospital. I looked at him in despair, and asked, 'Does that mean I've got to see him?'

'No,' he replied. 'But if you agreed to see him just the once he might not come again.'

'Do you mean to say he's been here before?' I asked.

He confirmed this was true, that Dad had been at the hospital a few times. The doctor had told him they didn't think it best for me to see him just yet, in case it interfered with the treatment they were giving me.

He went on to say that if I agreed to see Dad this time it might satisfy Dad's curiosity and that the doctor would be in the room with us anyway. He also told me that he would only be allowed to stay for ten minutes.

Reluctantly, I agreed, wishing Mum and Tony were with me.

As I followed him to his office I suddenly realised that this was the first time I could remember that I would be seeing my father on my own. In the past Mum had always been with me, and the very thought terrified me. I felt I wanted to run, but instead I carried on walking behind the doctor. All I wanted was to take a handful of pills – how I yearned for them.

The doctor pushed open the door and there in front of me sat Dad. All the horrible memories of the past, and the hate I felt for him, built up inside me in that split second. He got up from his chair and walked over to me with his arms outstretched. He took me in his arms and as he cuddled me I thought to myself, 'You rotten bastard.' I couldn't help it, I just hated him so much. I stood there rigidly with no emotion showing. But he was blind to the fact that I found him repellent and had no idea what he had done to make me feel that way.

I could smell the drink on his breath and clothes but thought it best to say nothing which might upset him. I hated him, but I also feared him just as much. Those ten minutes seemed a lifetime and because I felt so frightened of him I didn't really hear or take any notice of what he was saying to me. I just kept looking at the clock on the wall behind him, praying for the minutes to go as quickly as possible.

Eventually, the doctor told Dad he would have to leave. Without any argument Dad got up and said, 'Yes, of course.' He then looked at me and said, 'I promise to see you again, Ann,' and gave me a hug.

Not if I can help it, I thought to myself and the doctor saw him out.

I flopped down on the chair, knowing I could never go through that again. The shock of it all suddenly hit me and I started shaking. I heard the door open again, it made me jump. I turned round, but it was only the doctor coming back in.

'Are you all right?' he asked.

'Well, I wish you hadn't suggested I see him,' I said. 'Is it all right if I go now?' I asked, and with that I left the office.

I was so angry that I had had to go through that experience and was still trembling as I remembered Dad's last words, 'I promise to see you again.'

The words kept going round and round in my head, haunting me. Tony was due to visit soon and I couldn't wait to tell him what had happened. I always felt safe with him and I felt sure he wouldn't let Dad near me again. I told Tony all about it and the dreadful effect it had on me, so he made an appointment to see the doctor. The doctor told us both that I would not have to see Dad again if that was my choice. However, the fear didn't leave me and that night I couldn't sleep for thinking about it. I was so distressed and restless that the nurse rang the doctor who, in turn, gave her permission to give me some strong sleeping pills. After taking the pills I felt the fear slowly leaving me and was so relieved that I had been given them because I found they gave me strength. To be honest, they gave me the same wonderful feeling as the slimming pills that I was in hospital to be cured of. Was there any chance that I had found a substitute pill which would take away the pain and anguish of life? I might have been cured of one drug but by some fluke they might have prescribed a different drug which I could very well become addicted to. I didn't care what the name of it was or what its purpose was, just as long as it took the edge off my despair.

Although I was an in-patient, I had a lot of freedom and was permitted to come and go as I pleased. There was no problem going out to the shops or seeing Tony, or doing anything else that I wanted to do. Obviously I had to be back in time for my evening meals and let them know where I was, but I was more or less a free agent.

I liked the effects the sleeping pills had on me and made up my mind that if they were going to make life easier for me to cope with, then I would plump for them. It was incredibly easy to get them and this time I didn't have to forge any prescriptions, because all I needed to do was to tell the nurse I couldn't sleep and the doctors wrote out prescriptions. They were private doctors so I had to pay for the drugs, but that was no problem either. I used to make up excuses to Tony whenever I needed the money and he gave me whatever I asked for without hesitation.

I didn't like doing it but it was the only way I could escape the fear that was eating away at me. After six months I was living half of the time at the hospital and the other half at home.

It was during the latter part of this period that I became pregnant with my first child. I was both surprised and delighted at the idea of having a child of my very own. I had the task of telling Tony he was about to be a father again; after all, he already had three children by his wife. I hoped he would be as happy as I was and, come to think of it, would Mum be able to accept it?

The time came when I knew I had to tell him, and when he took me back to the hospital one night, I said, 'Tony, I've got something to tell you. I'm pregnant and I want to keep the baby, so before you say anything I thought I'd let you know how I feel.' It all came out just like that in one breath. I was praying he would agree with me to have the child. For a moment Tony looked stunned and didn't say a word, and I suppose I couldn't blame him really, for it came as such a surprise to both of us. We had never planned anything like this. He turned to look at me and still remained silent.

This was driving me mad so I said, 'Aren't you going to say anything, then?' and his reply was, 'Oh Ann, I do love you. Of course I want our baby, but what on earth's your Mum going to say?'

'Don't worry, I'll tell her,' I said and with that he gave me a kiss and I got out of the car and called out 'Good-night' as I entered the hospital doors. Telling Mum was the least of my problems. I could manage that all right and I felt sure she would welcome a baby of ours, but I found it difficult to face the doctor. After giving it considerable thought, I decided to inform the doctor in writing. I sat at a table and wrote the letter to him. It was easier to write as opposed to telling him face to face. I addressed the envelope and went to bed. The following day was a Saturday and I was due home, so I pushed the letter under the door of his office. On the way home Tony was a bit nervous. He was worried about what Mum would say about the baby. We arrived home and I told him to vanish for a while to give me a chance to have a word with Mum on my own.

I sat down and told Mum to sit next to me as I had something important to tell her. I told her I was expecting a baby, and at first she said nothing.

The first thing she did was ask if I wanted the baby and I said, 'Oh, yes, Mum. I want the baby so much,' and Mum looked at me and smiled. She leant over to me and gave me a big cuddle and in a way I knew she was pleased with my decision.

That night Mum said she was thinking it might be best for us to find somewhere else to live, as Dad knew our present address and, now that the baby was on its way, it would be better if we could find a house of our own. Shortly afterwards she found a lovely house in South Harrow that she liked and, whilst I was in hospital awaiting the birth of the baby, Tony helped her move. Life looked good for all of us. On 13 July 1962 my first child was born. The nurse laid my beautiful daughter in my arms and I cried with joy. The first thing I did was to examine her little pink body, making sure she had all her toes and fingers. She was perfect and I was so happy. I was very tired after the delivery but, as I looked down at my baby, my only prayer was that her life would be blessed and that it would have much smoother sailing than mine. I held her close and whispered to her so many promises. I had so many plans and ambitions for her and wanted her to know how much I loved and wanted her. That night Tony and Mum came to see her for the first time. Like many fathers, Tony didn't have much to say but looked admiringly at his new child. As Mum picked the baby up I could tell she was looking upon her as her own daughter. I knew Mum had missed out on my early years, and as my baby lay in Mum's arms I was pleased she had a grandmother with so much love to give to her.

I was nineteen, going on twenty now. I couldn't stop taking

the drugs. I had been able to obtain them quite easily and was addicted completely once more. Mum and Tony knew, but there was very little they could do to stop it.

Chapter 7

I slipped back to forging the prescriptions again. I honestly didn't want to keep taking the drugs and yet I couldn't survive without them. It was during this period that I tried to take my life on more than one occasion. I would accumulate pills and swallow the whole lot. Mum would find me sprawled out on the floor and rush me to hospital. This was hard on her, and I hate myself for doing it, for she had gone through hell herself. She helped me try to get back to normal, but I always returned to the view that I didn't want to live, I wanted out. I often put the gas on and simply lay there in front of it to inhale the fumes and on one occasion I can remember putting it on and placing a pillow in the oven. I put a row of photographs beside me of Tony, Mum and baby Karen. I took a couple of sleeping pills and lay perfectly still, but Mum and Tony found me in time.

Today I am glad I survived, but at the time I felt terrible. Nothing ever seemed to come easy and I was constantly fighting so much, whether it was with Dad or the pills. The final straw was that Tony and I were starting to have problems, too, for, although he was still attentive and gave me some support, the fact remained he was a married man.

It was around this time that justice caught up with me again as I was found out for forging prescriptions once more. I appeared in court and this time no pity was shown. I had been given many chances to be cured and none of them had worked. As I stood in court this time I was sentenced to Borstal. It was just two days before my twenty-first birthday.

As I left the courtroom and was shown to my cell I thought of the judge's words as he sentenced me. Two years seemed a lifetime and I didn't know that if I showed good behaviour I could expect to get out a lot sooner. As I sat alone in my cell, I just cried and cried. I couldn't bear to think I'd be away from my baby that long. My daughter was now thirteen months old and she had given me such happiness, even though I was drugged up with pills. What would Mum do, and would Tony wait for me? All these thoughts went through my mind as I sat there waiting for the police to take me to prison.

The key went in the door and the warden said, 'Come on, they're ready for you.'

She spoke sharply to me so I got up quickly because she frightened me a bit. I didn't really want to upset anyone and did as I was told. I followed her outside the building to where a big black van was parked. I learned later that it was a black Maria and as I climbed up the steps to get in even in my distressed state I noticed the row of small doors with mesh on the windows. The policeman who had taken me from the warden showed me which compartment to sit in. There was a small wooden seat and I sat down on it. The door shut and I heard the policeman lock it tight. As I looked at the partition in front of me I noticed there was writing on it. It read. 'I was here, 1963,' signed, 'Kathy'. The words had been scribbled in felt pen. I looked down at the floor and thought how clean it looked. I sat there sobbing my heart out with the magistrate's words, 'Two years!' ringing in my ears.

As I sobbed, I heard a gentle male voice trying to console me, saying, 'Hey, it'll be OK. It's not as bad as you think. I've been inside before and you'll be surprised how quickly the time goes.' He seemed so young and yet reassuring, and somehow it comforted me. I thanked him and he said, 'Believe me, I know. You'll get through it all right, you'll see.'

He made me feel a little bit better and made me realise I wasn't totally on my own.

Suddenly, I heard another man's voice call out, '*Ann!*' Is that you?'

I knew instantly it was my Dad. Of all the courts in England and of all the black Marias, he had to be in mine! Believe me, I wasn't laughing at the time. I still believed my father was capable of harming me, despite the fact that there was wire mesh between us, that the doors were locked, and that there

72

were police officers present. What could I say, except, 'Yes, Dad – it's me.'

He kept calling out my name. I thought fate was saying to me that I hadn't suffered enough yet.

My father shouted out, 'Don't worry, Ann. You wait till I get out! I'll see your mother and Tony and tell them I'm not having my daughter behind bars!'

There I sat, ashamed that I had put myself in a position where I was about to serve a prison sentence, and equally ashamed of my father, who did not know it was *he* who was the reason behind it all. I held my hands over my ears as I sat in my little compartment. There can't be many people who can't wait to get to prison, but that's how I felt. Anything, so long as I could get away from my father again. I prayed we'd reach my destination as soon as possible, so I could be locked up, safe from the man I had been terrified of all my life.

By the evening I was in such a state that I went berserk inside my prison cell. I started breaking up everything I could get my hands on. I shouted and yelled at the top of my voice until I was taken to the prison hospital, where I found the staff to be kind. My twenty-first birthday I spent all day in the workshop. One of the wardens came up to me with a posy in her hands, saying, 'Ann, would you like to see your family? They are waiting outside to see you. That is, of course, if you promise to be on your best behaviour.'

As the posy was from my daughter I was overjoyed, and eagerly agreed to control myself in order to see Karen and the others. I was taken to a special waiting room for visitors where Tony, Mum and my little girl were all waiting. They had sent me so many flowers that day, bunches and bunches of them. Nobody knew for sure how long I would be behind bars, although I had resolved that I would try my best not to aggravate the situation, that I would be an exemplary prisoner. Tony, Mum and Karen were asked to leave after half an hour and I continued my stay in Holloway for another week.

In that short time I made friends with a girl called Chris, and soon discovered that we were both waiting for our transfer to the same Borstal, Bullwood Hall. I had two major problems to face at this point: being able to cope without drugs, which was a terrible ordeal in itself, and not being allowed to smoke. I have always been since then, a heavy smoker.

The day arrived for us to be transferred. On arrival, we were shown into a huge hall which had rooms going all the way around the top of the landing, with stairs climbing to the landing itself. There was a large dining room to one side of the hall and I stood still for a moment, trying to take in the vast size of the building. I don't know precisely how many girls lived there at one time, but would hazard a guess at forty or fifty.

In spite of being upset about the predicament I was in I knew I had no option but to face up to reality and that I would have to somehow or other pull myself together. Chris and I were shown to our rooms and it was then, and only then, that I truly realised that my sentence had commenced.

Over the months that followed, Chris and I tended to stay with each other as much as possible and we found comfort in our friendship. The first couple of weeks went quite smoothly and I soon managed to get into a routine. I was always polite and friendly, as is my nature, but unfortunately not everyone reciprocated. On one occasion I was walking across the landing towards my room when a girl came up to me and, for no apparent reason, started hitting me. I knew I mustn't retaliate, for I was frightened that a brawl might put a stop to my coming home earlier than planned. There were no wardens anywhere near us, so all I could do was let her carry on attacking me, until eventually someone became aware of the disturbance and the wardens swooped down to investigate. They helped me back to my room where I panicked, anxious that I had hit the girl back, but they assured me I had no need to worry. After a while I learned the reason for the attack. I was ignorant of the fact that some women are lesbians and so I could not have guessed that my friendly overtures were being interpreted as an attempted seduction of my attacker's girlfriend. In time the aggressive girl came to apologise to me and the incident was over and forgotten. I shall never forget the date I was to be freed, it was 8 April 1964 and it couldn't come quickly enough.

Prior to my leaving, I was taken to the matron's room, where she told me that I was one of the few girls who had ever been allowed out of Borstal so early, which was due to my good behaviour and self-control. In total, I had spent seven long months in Bullwood Hall. There was another memorable incident which took place one Saturday evening. We used to have recreation downstairs in the big hall every Saturday evening, when we were allowed to play records and dance. On this particular night, I happened to be standing near the stairs. As I watched all the others enjoying themselves, I suddenly heard an almighty scream. It sounded as if it was coming from one of the rooms above. A warden who was on duty that evening was standing near to me and she also heard it, so we both tore upstairs to investigate.

We were the first to reach the room from where the screaming was coming. We barged open the door to find that the girl inside had tried to attract attention to herself by lighting the piles of newspapers which surrounded her. In the process, her nightdress had caught alight, and she suffered third-degree burns. Whilst the fire was being extinguished the wardens allowed some of us to go and console the poor girl until the ambulance arrived. The wretched sight of that girl's face and limbs will stay with me for the rest of my life.

On the day I was to be released I sat on the stairs in the big hall feeling very glad to be able to wear my own clothes for the first time in seven months, instead of the awful uniform. Tony was unable to come up to drive me home so my Uncle Bill came to collect me, bringing with him Mum and baby Karen. My baby was now about twenty-one months old and I couldn't wait to see how she had grown.

I was incredibly excited as I sat waiting for them to arrive and, to make matters worse, they were late. When I saw my mother at the door I burst into tears. We walked out of the building towards my uncle's car. I sat in the back where my little girl was sitting. She looked even more beautiful than last time I saw her and had grown so much. She was more like a proper little girl now rather than a baby, I longed to cuddle and kiss her, but to my horror she didn't recognise me at all. I had been away from her for such a large part of her short life that I was a perfect stranger as far as she was concerned. Initially this hurt me very much, but once I remembered I was going home as a free woman, I tried to make the best of it. After all, it wouldn't take me long to get back into the swing of family life and then Karen would grow to love me and know me as her mother again.

Chapter 8

Tony had rented a house for us to live in together. He had left his wife permanently by now and we were able to set up home together for the very first time. For some reason my father had stopped coming round to see us. Years later, we heard through the grapevine that he had been very ill, then passed to spirit. Apparently, he had tried to get Mum to visit him during his illness, which I understand may have been cancer, but she refused to go. No one knows for sure how or where he died. After a rest I got a job that I really loved at a garage in West Harrow, it was good money because it was shift work. If I happened to finish my shift early in the afternoon, little Karen would run down from the top of our road to meet me, while Mum waited and watched us. On the whole, life was pretty good at this stage. My memories of the time I had spent in Borstal were gradually fading, although those of the pills were not. To have to face up to the world without them was extremely difficult, for I realised the truth was that I had found it much easier behind the closed doors of Borstal or hospital. Having to face the outside world was a terrifying proposition. It wasn't long before I felt the desire to take drugs again so I started taking pep-up pills, which I bought over the counter at the local chemist's.

I soon found that they just weren't strong enough for my needs. I had put on a lot of weight during my stay in Borstal, so one day I plucked up the courage to visit a general practitioner, saying that I wished to diet and I had been prescribed slimming pills in the past for that reason. The doctor was very obliging and gave me a prescription without hesitation. Little did he know what he had done. That was the start of my becoming addicted again.

It was quite easy for me to obtain repeat prescriptions from him, and then from other doctors, and I found it much easier than before to get the pills without having to forge them. This time I had become more cunning, as I vowed I would never go back to prison, and so I found several different doctors who agreed to take me on as a private patient. Very soon I was seeing three doctors a week, which made it even easier to obtain repeat prescriptions, and each doctor was unaware of what I was up to. This pattern was to become part of my life in the years to come.

Tony was waiting for his divorce to be finalised and not long after I came out of Borstal I felt I really wanted another baby. I became pregnant that same year and continued working at the garage. We then moved into a flat in Welldon Crescent, Harrow. My second pregnancy was well on the way when we learned that my cousin Joyce and her husband were having problems with their marriage. They had two small children, a son, then aged two and a half, and a daughter of six months. I had always envied Joyce her lot in life since she seemed to have everything that I had never had. Although she had lost her mother at an early age, and she hadn't seen her father for years, she nevertheless always looked well-groomed and attractive and wore lovely expensive clothes. She and her husband lived in a beautiful flat and she was adored by her near-perfect spouse. When we heard that she and her husband were having problems the news came as a bit of a shock. One morning, in the following March, I was in our flat with Karen whilst Mum was out shopping, when there was a knock at the door. When I answered the door my Uncle Eddie was standing there, asking to see my mother. When I told him she was out he said that he would pop back later and stressed there wasn't anything for me to worry about. Two hours later he returned to speak to my mother, announcing that Joyce was dead.

He had the presence of mind not to tell me when I was on my own that morning as I was carrying my second child and Joyce and I were not only cousins but we were also quite close friends. She had been found early that morning, having committed suicide. That same day I vowed I would never be jealous of anyone again, and I never have been. Nobody knows what goes on behind closed doors, do they? I also vowed that if I had another daughter I would name her Joyce. Joyce was only twenty-two years old when she died and my younger daughter was born on 1 May 1965, two months later.

Even though we were feeling the sadness of Joyce's untimely death, we now had two little girls, a tremendous joy to us all. In my eyes my family was now complete and I was happy, despite the fact that I was still suffering from ill-health. For the first time in many years I felt at peace, for Dad, God rest his soul, was no longer around to intimidate us and I had two beautiful daughters. We lived in the same flat for about eighteen months and I went back to work at the garage, whilst Mum stayed at home to look after the two children. I was able to cope with my job and the drugs at the same time.

In time we moved on once again, this time to a bigger flat in Pinner Road and we lived there for three years. The make of slimming pill I was addicted to was being withdrawn from the market, but I found out that a new sleeping pill was available on prescription. I acted on this information straight away, getting prescriptions from general practitioners for the new drug by paying for them.

We lived in our large flat until I was twenty-seven. Mum continued to look after the children whilst Tony and I went out to work. We had our ups and downs, like all families, but then my drug addiction was beginning to take its toll. Mum and Tony were well aware what I was doing to my body that there was no hope of my ever coming off drugs. They had to contend with changes of mood and tantrums and took each day as it came.

One morning my mother woke up feeling very ill. She had suffered a massive stroke in the night. We rushed her to hospital and for the next four weeks she fought with all her might. The doctors told me that Mum had had such a severe stroke at her age because of the beatings she had endured years ago. She had very strong willpower, something which was made clear to me one afternoon when I went to visit her in hospital. She could hardly see and yet she was sitting up, trying to pretend she was reading a book as she waited for the doctor to come to examine her. She was equally determined to come home to the two children she absolutely adored. Four weeks later she was allowed to come home. The doctors gave her a walking stick for support but as she walked out of the door she threw it away. It took her many months to get back on her feet, and from that time on she had several periods of illness, but, being a woman with such a strong constitution, she fought them all.

Once Mum was well on the road to recovery, Tony and I began to go through a rough patch. We decided to break up. We needed breathing space away from each other and I moved into a house near to the garage where I worked. On reflection, I now blame the drugs, for they made me do so many strange things. I used to say very hurtful things to him, blurting them out before thinking what I was saying, things I would never have said had I not been under the influence.

I took Mum and the children with me and we stayed there for a whole year. It was whilst we lived at this house that I met an American. What I didn't know was that history would repeat itself. I fell in love with the American – he was so full of fun, laughter, life – and shortly after meeting him I decided to live with him. Mum thought it wasn't a good idea for all of us to go, so she stayed in the house and I looked in every day, keeping an eye on her and the girls. He beat me senseless, although I didn't fully realise it at the time because, along with the drugs, I was now drinking as well. I lived with him for about five months in all and then he wanted to take me to Spain with him for a holiday. Tony was still in the shadows, he never wanted to part from me completely, and many a time he and Mum had to collect me from the hospital following a beating I had sustained from my American. Yet, despite their desperate attempts at trying to make me see sense and leave him, love is blind and at that time it was the last thing I wanted to do. They begged me not to go to Spain with him for they could see him for what he was, but I wouldn't listen.

I started going to spiritualist churches in the area on the

occasional Sunday and I happened to go to one the week before we were due to fly out to Spain. The medium came to me and advised me not to go because I would live to regret it. Even then I refused to listen and, as I came out of the church, I insisted to my friends that I still intended going as it was the first chance I had of a holiday in my lifetime, and so I chose to ignore what the spirit world had told me. If only we took their advice, but we rarely do, I'm sorry to say.

Before I went to Spain, Mum, the children and Tony decided to live together again for Tony's mother had died, leaving him a house in Long Lane, Hillingdon. I set off for Spain with my American. I was arrogant and selfish at that time and thought I knew best, but I very soon found out the hard way that I should have listened to everyone who tried to put me off going. We had only been there for a day and a half, maybe two days, when he went berserk. He tried to strangle me until I passed out.

The following morning I awoke to find myself sprawled out across the sofa. I don't know how, but I managed to pick myself up and make for the bathroom. I was all aches and pains and found it difficult to walk, but when I looked at my face in the mirror I was horrified. I was so scared I ran out to see some people whom we had briefly befriended on arrival and they helped me to catch the first plane back home. Tony met me at London Airport at five o'clock in the morning. I was in a terrible state by the time I reached the airport. Half my hair was missing, I was black and blue and in desperate need of drugs. He took me straight to the doctor, who prescribed sleeping pills. Then he shepherded me back to the house in Hillingdon. It was there I steadily relapsed into sickness and depression until the time came when I felt that I could no longer cope.

I tried to commit suicide again, by taking a large overdose and was rushed to hospital and put on open order. The doctors there told Mum and Tony that if I didn't pull through by seven o'clock that evening then I wouldn't make it at all. Looking back, I think I must have had an extraordinary amount of help and support, not only from the people in this world, but the next one, too. Sheer hell is what Mum and Tony were going through and I shudder when I think it was all my fault. They didn't deserve the life they lived with me, including all my attempts at taking my own life, not to mention my black moods and screaming fits. They say you always hurt the one you love, and that is so true.

I spent a whole month in hospital following the last failed attempt at suicide and when I came out Tony and I decided to get married. I was twenty-eight by now and Tony's divorce had been finalised. We had overcome our problems and now he was free to marry me. We were both very happy with our decision as we felt ready to commit ourselves to each other and seal our love properly.

We lived in Long Lane for a few years and when I was better I went back to work. I was still a drug addict as I found it quite easy to get the pills I needed, repeating the pattern of paying two or three independent doctors each week for repeat prescriptions. This kept me going, but it wasn't long before I became terribly ill again. As I look back I see that all I was doing was imitating my father. The only difference between him and me was the thin dividing line between physical and mental cruelty.

I gradually became more and more desperate, praying to God that I wouldn't wake up each morning. If only I could die – it would stop all the misery I was causing. The more misery I could see I was creating, the more pills I took, and the more pills I took, the more misery I inflicted on my loved ones. I might be fine for a few weeks, or even a few months, but then Tony and Mum would see the warning lights and keep a close watch on me in case I would try to do anything rash again. I woke up very early one morning and I saw vividly two nuns praying at the bottom of my bed. I lay there looking at them, hardly daring to move, put my head under the sheets and went back to sleep. I told Mum and Tony when I eventually got up, but they thought it was my imagination. But that was the very first time I saw spirit. Although it came unexpectedly it didn't really frighten me, if anything it seemed to have a calming influence. To tell the truth, it didn't really make much of an impression on me at the time, but when another incident occurred which concerned spirit I took more notice. It happened a few years after my cousin Joyce died and it was the first time I was fully aware of spirit being around me. I had had a dream that Joyce was at the front door. When I went to answer it we ran into each other's arms, crying.

When I got up the morning after my vivid dream I told my mother about it and she said that she had heard crying all night long. She added that the crying was so loud that she had actually gone to all the bedrooms to see who it was who was obviously so upset, but found us all fast asleep. Every night for a week Mum was tormented by the crying noise, but only she ever heard it. Mum had never believed in there being a spirit world, but nevertheless called in a priest. The priest came and carried out an exorcism and Mum confirmed that the crying ceased after that.

Many years later I learnt that it was Joyce telling us that she had been very unhappy towards the end of her life. Apparently even the priest thought this might be the case, which is something to think about.

I was rapidly becoming more sick when we decided to move just down the road to another house. I was finding it increasingly difficult to move my hands and fingers and had to ask my eldest daughter to write a cheque out for me one day because I found it hard to hold the pen, let alone write the words on it. Although the pills had taken their toll I was still working. My daughter Karen was now coming up to fourteen, a vulnerable and impressionable age. At the time I had no idea how awful it must have been for her to have a mother swaying from side to side at the top of the stairs and not letting her have friends in her own home. I learnt later that my mother always used to make sure I was either in bed or out of the way before Karen brought anyone home. My younger child, Joyce, must have wondered why her mother was different from the mothers of her friends. Karen had her first boyfriend at fifteen, at a time when I knew I was desperately ill and yet could do nothing to stop it, even though I could see the terrible effect it was having on my family. I would lie in bed, doped up to the eyeballs, demanding Karen's time and attention. I knew in my heart that I loved her, and yet here I was showing her up, embarrassing her in front of her friends. Eventually I found I couldn't go out to work any more. It was then that Mum decided the best thing to do was for her to take the girls away to live apart from Tony and me. I was so drugged up at the time I didn't have a clue what was going on, but the social services had been to see my mother and put the children under her care. It was the right thing to do for them.

Chapter 9

Tony and I sold the house and bought a mobile home in Denham. Mum and the kids settled into their new home but I didn't like being away from the girls and Mum. The decision to make the break almost broke my heart, for it was almost as if half of me had been taken away. Whilst we lived in our mobile home I didn't see Mum or the girls every day, for I knew it would do them more harm than good. The younger one was at school anyway and the elder out at work, so I decided to visit them at Mum's house on Saturdays only. However, every time I turned up Karen would turn her back on me, even if she had a friend with her. She would make it abundantly clear that she wanted nothing to do with me and this treatment hurt me badly. I tried everything I could think of to win her back, including money. On the day we received the money from the sale of the house we went to the bank. I felt I had to give the children something of it, so straight away we drew some money out to give them both. When we arrived at Mum's house we found Mum was out shopping but both girls were at home. I had one thousand pounds in my pocket and I admit I was trying to buy Karen's love and attention.

As Joyce opened the front door she smiled and I knew she loved me by the way she looked at us, and for that I was truly grateful to God. With Mum, she had tried so hard to help me and had never turned her back on me.

The Easter holidays had just finished and Joyce had given me an Easter card. She had signed her name on the bottom of it and had forged her sister's name so I would think that both of them had sent it. But I knew only too well how bitter Karen was towards me, as I had been towards my father. All of these thoughts went through my head as I walked into the living room. Karen was sitting on the settee reading a book.

'Hello,' I said.

There was no reply. As I sat down I said to Joyce, 'Here is five hundred pounds for you. Put it away safely in a bank account. Your grandmother knows I've given it to you,' and I handed over the money.

Looking over to Karen, I said quietly, 'And here's your five hundred pounds.'

No other words were spoken and I had to get up and go before I started to cry. Karen hadn't even looked at me, so I said before I left, 'Joyce, give this to her, please,' and with that I gave her a kiss and left. Tony was sitting in the car. 'Don't try to buy her,' he said. 'You'll have to wait till she's ready.'

'That's easier said than done,' I replied, feeling choked up inside. I just couldn't explain how I felt and how could a man possibly know how I felt?

As he drove I sat in silence. Would she ever understand that I had never meant to harm her?

When we arrived back home I sat Tony down in front of me and said to him, 'I can't go on, Tony,' and tears filled my eyes. 'I don't want to take my life but I wish God would take me instead. What point is there in me being here?'

I was feeling too selfish to realise that Tony loved me and needed me. I went on, 'I feel I desperately need help but I don't know what sort of help.'

Tony looked up at me. Both he and Mum had tried everything within their power to help me, but to no avail. How could he help me just that little bit more now? Tony had always tried to help me find the pills I needed and his determination to help me in whatever way I wanted had eventually broken down the strong friendship he had always had with Mum. Tony was the only one who could keep tabs on my actions and a tight control over the pills I had in my possession. It would be the only way he could prevent me from killing myself. I felt sorry for Tony to have to go through this with me, and I felt sorry for the others, too. All I had ever done in my life was to bring pain to my loved ones and I couldn't see an end to it in the future.

As I sat there with my hands covering my face, a thought came into my head. Perhaps if I went to church I could get some help or guidance there. Anything, as long as I could change the look on my daughter's face every time she saw me and take away the hate she felt towards me. Looking up, I said to Tony, 'Will you take me to church?'

He looked surprised, for it was something I had never asked him to do before.

'Oh, please, Tony,' I begged. 'Will you take me to one now?'

'Yes,' he replied, 'but which one do you want to go to?'

I told him to take me to a Roman Catholic church, but I didn't care which one, I just felt I needed to go.

Tony got up and went out to the car. I got my coat and before I knew it I could hear Tony tooting the car horn to let me know he was ready. I quickly checked I had the keys to the door safely in my handbag and I walked out, shutting the door behind me. It was cold, not the best of nights to go out in, but I was determined to go to church no matter what. I wasn't quite sure what it was I was searching for and I am sure Tony didn't know either, but whatever else I felt I needed to pray. We drove around the streets for a little while until we came across the church. Tony pulled up outside and asked me, 'Do you want me to come in with you, Ann?'

'No, I'd rather go in on my own if you don't mind.' I leant over to him and gave him a kiss. 'Stop worrying about me, love. I just need to go into the church for a short time, that's all,' I said.

Hugging me, Tony said, 'I just hope you find what you are looking for,' and he smiled at me.

I said, 'I hope so, too,' and got out of the car.

As I walked up the stone steps towards the doors my stomach was churning. I wondered if I was being silly, if the priest would understand my predicament. All manner of thoughts went through my mind; above all was the thought of my children and the impression I had on them and their attitudes towards me. We had been a united family for years and now we were divided. I couldn't get the look in my elder child's eyes out of my mind and I sincerely hoped the priest would be able to help me.

As I pushed the door open I could see many people kneeling in prayer inside the vast church. The priest was in the distance and it was evident that he was carrying out a service, so I moved quietly towards the back of the church, finding a tranquil spot to sit and wait for the priest to finish. I felt so cold as I sat there and where I was sitting was very dark. I shivered for a moment, scared, not of the church itself but of the priest. I had been brought up in the Catholic faith so I knew there was nothing to be frightened of, but it was now the first time for many years since I had been to church. I pulled my coat round my trembling body and hoped the service would soon be over.

Eventually, as it came to a close, I sat and watched the people get up from their pews and walk past me to go out. One lady smiled at me so I smiled back but my mind was on the priest. He came down from the pulpit and entered a small room at the side of the church. I got up and walked towards the small room. The door was open and I could see the priest taking off his robe over his head. I knew I shouldn't have imposed upon him but I was so desperate that I barged in.

'Yes, can I help you?' he asked.

I rushed into the room and knelt down in front of the priest, crying like a banshee. 'Please, please help me!' I wailed. I tried to explain my circumstances to him in between sobs, but the more I tried to tell my story, the more tears came.

His answer cut through me like a knife.

'Do not be a silly child. Go home to them and they will forgive you.'

He made the sign of the cross above my head and said he had to go. I thanked him and slowly got up off my knees. I felt totally numb as I walked out of the little room, through the church, and as I approached the doors I stopped. I turned round and looked back towards the altar where a large figure of Jesus Christ on the cross stood high and magnificent.

'Thanks,' I mumbled under my breath and, to be perfectly honest, wondered what the hell I was doing there. I was angry.

As I reached the door I vowed I would never kneel to another human being on this earth. I pushed the door open and the cold air hit me once again. I wrapped my coat around me to keep warm and from where I was standing I could see Tony. He had seen my shadow through the doorway and had already got out of the car, and was now standing at the foot of the steps, looking up at me. Very slowly he walked up the steps towards me whilst I just stood there, holding my coat close to me. Perhaps I had gone inside in the hope of finding a miracle, maybe hoping someone or something could show me the way, but instead I felt more lost and more confused. I felt no warmth or comfort whatsoever but was left to feel cold and numb. I felt Tony's hand in mine as he said, 'Come on, love, let's go home.'

When we got to the car Tony looked at me enquiringly. 'Has it helped you, Ann?' he asked as he unlocked the car door on my side.

I leant forward to open the car door and got in. Tony walked round the back of the car and got in his side. He started the car. I couldn't answer him, mainly because I didn't have an answer. I didn't really know what I was expecting when I went into that church but I certainly did think I would have had some kindness and consideration shown to me.

I sat in total silence until we reached our mobile home. I had been hurt deep within and I just wanted to be left alone.

'Do you mind if I go to bed?' I asked Tony as soon as we got in.

All Tony said was, 'I presume it didn't help then.'

I turned my head away as I could feel the tears coming again.

'No, it didn't,' I cried, and with that went to bed.

As I lay in bed I thought about the Church's teaching that God is always with us. Well, where were you tonight, God? The question remained unanswered when I fell fast asleep.

The following morning nothing was said about the visit

to the church and I tried to put it all at the back of my mind. I decided to visit a doctor to tell him or her of my drug addiction. After breakfast we set off and managed to find a lovely lady doctor who was willing to take me on as her patient. She warned me that she was going to let every doctor in the area know she was treating me so I wouldn't be able to go to any other doctor for pills. I accepted this as I wanted to prove to my family that I could make good and maybe one day take that look out of my daughter's eyes. I had tried so many times before to come off the pills and had always failed, but this time I knew I had to make it or die, for I was very ill. I was slowly wasting away but, besides that, I was losing my family.

So, slowly but surely, I started coming off the pills. It was very difficult and there were days when I would have loved to have died. If it hadn't been for the support of Mum and Tony I would have given in easily. Mum telephoned me every day and Tony was always with me. The battle was hard and there was a time when I couldn't handle it and I got some pills and tried to take my life. I was pulled out of it in the nick of time and went back to trying to cut down. One Sunday, I had had a really bad day when I found the effort of coming off the pills was too much to bear. I lay in bed that morning wondering, Why can't I just leave this earth or is that too much to ask? Every time I had tried taking my life in the past I had always been found in time by Mum or Tony, no matter how clever I had thought I had been. I was so unhappy but, more than that, I was making my family desperately unhappy and it was apparent to me that it wasn't worth them having me around any more to increase their unhappiness. I know that I was feeling particularly sorry for myself that day but I just couldn't help it and no matter how hard Tony tried I couldn't snap out of it.

'Come on, love, I'll tell you what we'll do today,' he said. 'We'll go to a different church tonight and see if that helps you at all. We haven't been to a spiritualist church for years and there's no harm in trying. What do you think? You never know, you might even get a message that will cheer you up and give you some hope to carry on. You've come this far and I can't bear seeing you like this.'

As Tony said, I hadn't been to a spiritualist church for a long time, but after the last visit to a church I felt it pointless to turn to God again.

'No, we'll leave it,' I said to Tony. 'I've really given up hope that turning to the Church will help after what happened the last time.'

As I looked at Tony I knew he thought I was going to give up trying to come off the pills. 'Look love,' I said. 'I don't want to go backwards, but I feel so unhappy because every time I try to come off them there seems to be an obstacle in my way and I can't see myself ever making it.'

'Well,' said Tony, 'it's no good having a go at you, Ann, we've all tried that in the past but if obstacles are there, surely you've got to try and get over them.'

'But I'm tired of trying,' I said. 'All I seem to do is hurt everyone around me, including myself.' I shrugged my shoulders in despair. I was too depressed to argue any more.

'Well, said Tony, "I'm going to the spiritualist church tonight, so it's up to you whether you want to come or not.'

He was well aware I hated being on my own so I said, 'OK, I'll go. Look, it's just a bad day for me but I still want to come off the pills.'

He smiled and said, 'I'm glad, Ann. Think of the girls.'

That's all I keep doing, I thought to myself.

The day dragged on and by the time we had to get ready to go my head was aching. I felt dreadful but I had to make the effort for Tony's sake. As I walked into the living room, Tony asked me if I was going to put some make-up on. I was taken aback by this as I very rarely used make-up and said so. 'Well, it's only that you look so pale and your eyes are red from crying,' he said.

I agreed and went back into the bedroom. As I sat down in front of the mirror I noticed how my face was looking drawn and, as I started putting my face powder on, I suddenly thought how old I was looking. I was only thirty-seven years old but the face looking back at me looked at least ten years older. I quickly powdered my face and got up. I felt depressed enough, without that!

When Tony saw me he told me I looked a lot better, thank goodness.

We left with plenty of time to spare before the church opened so we took a slow ride. I sat quietly with Tony asking me now and again if I was feeling all right. I would have replied 'Yes' but inside me I felt far from all right. As we drew up outside the church I felt like saying. 'Take me home,' but kept quiet. We were still a bit early so we sat in the car. I lit a cigarette and looked at the small church, wondering to myself what was the point in going inside. As I took another puff on my cigarette I remembered the times I had been to a spiritualist church before. I had been purely to receive messages from the other world about what the future had in store for me. The churches themselves had been unimportant. As we were sitting there I noticed lots of people going in so I looked at my watch. It was twenty-five past six and Tony said, 'Come on, love, we had better go in before they start the service. It begins in five minutes.'

I leant forward and put my cigarette out and said, 'OK' and got out of the car. I waited for Tony to lock the car and as I waited I thought how cold it was and yet the weather that day had been hot. Maybe it was me, I thought, as I wrapped my jacket around me. We walked into the little building and I could see how packed it was. We managed to find two seats at the back of the church and sat down.

The service commenced promptly and the medium was introduced. She was a very pleasant lady in her fifties or sixties. My mind, however, wasn't really on what she was saying, nor anything else that may have been going on around me; I could not snap out of my depression. After the prayers, hymns, healing silence and address, the medium stood up to give clairvoyance to the congregation and by this time I was at my lowest ebb. All I could think of was, Would someone please tell me I am going to die soon. I could feel the tears welling up in my eyes so I just bit my lip as I didn't want people to see me crying. I was sitting near a window and I started to look out of it. Suddenly, a voice was saying, 'I'm talking to you, love.' Tony nudged me and as I turned to him I could see the medium standing in front of me. I had been in a daze and hadn't heard her. Even as she was talking to me my mind went blank, but the words I had been thinking about came back into my mind and without thinking I just stood up. Tears that I had kept at bay whilst I had been sitting there suddenly started to flow, and with the tears now flowing down my cheeks, I interrupted her. 'Please can you tell me when I am going to die?'

I heard Tony gasp and I knew instantly I had made a complete fool of myself. I got up and rushed past Tony and out of the church to the car, forgetting that he had locked it. I couldn't go back to ask for the keys so I decided to walk up the road a bit.

Just then, I heard Tony call out, 'Ann, wait!'

I stopped in my tracks and turned round. As I watched him walking towards me I felt so ashamed for showing him up in front of all those people, and as he reached me I apologised.

'Come on, it doesn't matter,' he said and as we walked slowly back to the car I said to him that I really should go back and apologise to the medium.

'I agree,' said Tony, 'But I'm sure she understands.'

As we reached the car people were coming out of the little church and a couple of them came up to ask me how I was feeling now. They seemed genuinely concerned and both of them asked us to go back into the church for some tea. Tony agreed that it would be a good idea so we started to walk back in.

As we entered the doorway I stood still.

'Come on,' said the lady, 'everyone in there has a problem or is worried about something or other and they all understand.'

Her words gave me much comfort and I followed them in.

It didn't take me long before I found the medium, and, taking her to one side, I told her how sorry I was to behave in such a manner, and I hoped she would understand. She put her arms around me and gave me a kiss on the cheek.

'You are amongst friends now, my dear,' she said softly. 'And God will help you. You will see that in the years to come, I can promise you that.'

I thanked her and went to sit down next to Tony, who was talking to some other people, and my eyes went round the church itself. As I took stock of the people inside its walls I felt they were sympathetic to my plight, or at least they showed some interest or tried to. Most of them made me feel that I was not on my own in my distressed condition and that they, too, had at some time or another experienced my grief and pain in their own fashion. No one appeared to be in a hurry to leave, nor too busy to spare the time to show me they cared. My mind went back to the Catholic church where I was given the distinct impression that nobody cared, least of all God, and yet here, in this small, modest church, I had found friends and a door which was forever open, and no gold or glitter on show. It had no priest dressed in fine robes who was in too much of a hurry to listen but a whole body of people with one mind, all with the same belief that God Is Love, and that love is the key to life itself.

Although it was just a very small hut, not even made of bricks and mortar, there was such a beautiful atmosphere within the church and it caressed me, making me feel secure and protected by all the love that filled it. There was an altar table at one end, surrounded by fresh flowers and candles. There were piles of blue hymn books neatly stacked after the service and an old piano to one side of the church which also had vases of flowers on top of it. The tables were covered with clean, lacy tablecloths and there were more vases full of flowers everywhere I looked. The walls were covered with pictures of Jesus Christ and the main centrepiece was a simple wooden cross. As I looked at the cross I felt that God had not left me after all and that I had found Him again.

When we were on our way home, Tony asked me if I

was feeling any better. 'Oh, yes, love, much better,' and yet somehow I couldn't tell him why. Everyone had made me welcome and I felt as if a great weight had been lifted from my shoulders. For the first time in my life I felt I had found a haven, a sanctuary, where hands stretched out to give me the help and support I so badly needed, and I grabbed them as tightly as I possibly could with my own hands.

I continued to cut down on the pills but found I couldn't stay in the mobile home any longer – it was driving me up the wall – so we relocated to a house back in Hillingdon where we still live to this day. The uprooting marked a turning-point in my life. When we returned to Hillingdon I was down from twenty to only four pills a day, and I was able to take up work again. Karen was tentatively communicating with us again, which was marvellous. The family as a whole were all trying very hard to pick up the pieces, but nobody wanted to try harder than me. Although Mum and Tony knew I had managed to reduce my daily intake of pills, I don't think they honestly believed it possible for me to be completely cured. In my own heart, I never thought it possible either, but at least I was finally on the road to progress and beginning to feel partly normal again after such a long time. I had been to hell and back and had dragged my family behind me all the way, but I was now able to see the light at the end of the tunnel at last and hoped all was not lost. I was realising, too, that I had a chance of regaining my daughter's respect and I didn't want anything to prevent that from happening.

But I was still terrified of life. I didn't really know in what direction I was heading, nor if I really wanted to come off the four pills completely. As far as I was concerned, four pills a day didn't seem as bad as twenty. I was coping much better with Mum having the kids with her and I enjoyed going to see them, so in a way, it didn't seem as if we were really separated at all.

It was basically the drugs that had warped my vision, I know that now, yet I think coming to this house made it easier for me somehow. I still wasn't quite ready to reject the pills completely because until this point I hadn't won any battles. On the other hand, I had the two most beautiful daughters in the world, the best mother anyone could ever wish for, and a gem of a husband who had proved his love to me a thousand times over. I had been such a bitch to them during my trials and tribulations and he was, and still is, a tower of strength to me. All of them had stuck by me, but what had I done for them in return? What could I do for them now? That was the burning question. I would never have deliberately put them through hell had the drugs not overtaken and ruined my life. I loved them all far too much for that. People could quite easily say to me 'Well, nobody put the pills into your mouth. You did it, nobody forced you.' But I started to believe that it had all been fated from the very beginning.

We moved into the house in August and in September, to my utter amazement, I found I was pregnant. The doctors did not want me to have my baby because they feared I would not be able to handle both cutting the dosage of drugs and the pressures of having a new baby, and they argued that I should have an abortion. I wasn't at all sure about this, as I wanted both the baby and to be cured of drugs. Tony and I decided to ask a good friend of ours, who happens to be a medium, to consult the spirit world for us to ask their advice. The spirit does not order us, but they are here to help us, and they agreed with the doctor. After listening to both sides of the story Tony and I made the decision to go ahead with the termination. Looking at our two lovely daughters I could see the misery I had inflicted on them and, even though I was partly cured and wanted to keep the baby, I couldn't possibly put a third child of mine at risk.

The following months were spent settling down in our new home, visiting Mum and the girls. Life seemed to have returned to normal. Even my health was now much improved.

Little did I know that in the following spring something would happen that would completely change the whole course of my life.

Chapter 10

I woke up startled one morning and looked around me. Something had woken me but what it was I didn't know. I looked over at Tony, only to find he was blissfully sleeping. I looked at the clock and saw it was too early to get up so I lay back down, trying to get back to sleep. Whatever it was that had woken me had now vanished from my mind. The next thing I knew was Tony shouting in my ear, 'Ann, wake up!'

With my head in its usual position under the pillow, I shouted back, 'OK,' but really wishing he would just go away. Dragging myself out of bed, I walked into the bathroom and, as I washed myself, I suddenly felt, for some unknown reason, as if something or someone was with me. I turned round from the basin and had a good look round. Of course nothing was there so I turned back and carried on washing. I could hear Tony shouting at me to hurry up as he wanted to use the bathroom.

'I've finished!' I replied, and dashed into the bedroom to get dressed. Damn, I thought to myself, as I caught my tights. I could see the ladder running so I quickly found another pair and started to put them on. As I looked at my watch I thought, Good, I still have plenty of time before Tony drops me off at work. When I got downstairs I made a quick cup of tea and sat down to read the paper. Tony was still upstairs when I heard him shout out again, asking what the time was. I called the reply up to him and continued to read the paper. Just then, the feeling I had experienced in the bathroom was back. Looking up from the newspaper, I looked around me and a shiver went down my spine and then I felt cold.

I got up and called up to Tony, 'Tony, are you coming down yet?'

He said he had finished getting ready and that he'd be down

in a minute. I felt a bit foolish but I didn't want to be on my own in the room. When Tony came down the presence had gone and the feeling I had had gone, too. I smiled to myself, thinking, You're going doo-lally, Ann, and shrugged it off.

As, we drove to work I was thinking about how life was getting much better since we had moved from the mobile home. Karen and I were on better terms now and I was still very close to Joyce. I was on only four pills a day so, on the whole, things were much improved. We were very busy at work that day and the time went quickly, so by the time Tony came for me that night I was glad to get home. When we pulled up outside our house, and whilst Tony put the car away, I let myself into the house. As I entered the hallway I felt sure someone was in the house and the feeling I had that morning was back again, but this time much more strongly. I took my time, hoping Tony was coming.

'What's the matter?' he asked and as he stopped next to me I whispered, 'Ssh, I think there's someone in the house.'

'Hang on, I'll have a look,' Tony said in a quiet voice, with a glance as if he thought I was imagining things. He popped upstairs and then took a look around downstairs, then he said, 'It's all right.'

'Sorry, love,' I said, as I put my things down on the settee. Walking into the living room, he asked me what made me think there was someone there.

'I don't know.'

I hadn't mentioned my odd sensation that morning as it didn't seem that important, but the feeling I had then was now back. Tony didn't pursue it so I pushed it to the back of my mind. I turned the fire on.

'For God's sake, Ann,' Tony said when he saw what I was doing. 'You can't be cold!'

'Yes, I am!' I retorted, but I couldn't tell him why.

The following morning everything was fine and the incidents of yesterday were completely gone from my mind. Tony had arranged to pick me up at lunchtime from work as usual. I bought a few sandwiches from the baker's across the road and a bottle of drink ready for when Tony arrived. Sure enough,

Tony came for me dead on time and we took the old familiar route to the river. It was a lovely day, the sun shining. I was glad of the break as we had been busy again that morning at work. As he drove, Tony was talking about what had been going on at his work that morning and, as I listened to him, I started to eat one of my sandwiches. By the time we reached our usual spot I had finished my sandwiches and asked Tony to give me one of his because I was still hungry!

We parked the car when we got there and I laid my head back. I felt good for it was nice to get an hour off and relax. Tony had some papers from work with him and was looking over them. I just sat there enjoying the break, looking out of the window at the river which ran along my side of the car. It was only a small section of the river but nevertheless it was very pleasant. On the other side swans were sitting on the bank, enjoying the sunshine.

I turned to look at Tony, only to see him engrossed with his paperwork, so I looked at my watch and saw that we still had plenty of time. I looked back at the river, but this time, to my amazement, the view was entirely different from what I had seen before. What I could see now was a different river, one which had a bridge. A young boy of about eight or nine was walking across the bridge, kicking the sides of it with his shoes, and as he reached the other side of the bridge he found a tin can which he began to kick about. It was almost as if I could read his mind; he was very annoyed. At first I couldn't make out why he was so angry and then I realised that it was because his mother had bought him a new suit and the trousers were short. All his friends were now in long trousers and he wanted to be like all the others.

Suddenly I was conscious of Tony talking, but it seemed so far away. The scene with the little boy faded and I was now able to hear Tony clearly.

'Sorry, Tony, what did you say?' I asked him.

'Never mind, it wasn't that important, but where were you? You seemed to be miles away.'

I didn't answer him straight away because I wasn't sure what I had just witnessed. I knew it wasn't my imagination.

Also, I was puzzled as to who the young boy was. If I told Tony I knew he wouldn't laugh at me, for he isn't that sort of person, and he would listen to what I had to say.

I waited until he started the car and then I said, in a casual voice, 'Tony, I've got something to tell you. I've just seen something which I don't quite understand. Can I tell you about it?'

'Of course you can,' said Tony. I told him the whole story, wondering if it made any sense, not only to him, but maybe to me, also. Could Tony, with his enquiring mind, possibly have the answer? After I finished telling him everything he didn't say anything straight away. After a few minutes he asked me where and how I had got all the background information regarding the scene. My reply was, '*They* told me.'

'What do you mean by *they* told you? Who are *they* and why did *they* tell you?'

I thought about it for a moment, and then said, 'How do *I* know?'

I was getting more and more confused by Tony's attitude and questions, and annoyed with him because I had told him a simple story and expected a simple explanation. Instead of which I was getting the third degree.

'Was there anything else you saw?' he went on.

'No, not really,' I replied. 'Just what I told you, that's all.'

He stopped the car so I said, 'Come on, Tony, I'll be late back for work.'

I knew the other girl at work wouldn't be too annoyed if I was late back but I didn't like taking advantage of her good nature.

'Do you realise what you have just seen?' asked Tony.

I thought to myself, How would I know? I asked him what was bothering him and began to wish I had never spoken.

'I had better tell you,' said Tony. 'When I was eight or nine years old my mother bought me a suit as you described, and the bit about the river with the bridge going across it happened to me exactly as you told me. On the day in question *I* was wearing the new suit and it was *me* you saw kicking the tin can in anger. Every little detail you described to me was true, right down to the last detail, and yet when I asked you how you knew all this, all you said was that *they* were telling you. Is there no more? I can't make it out at all.'

'Tony, I really don't know how I know, I only know what I saw, that's all. Why I said *they* were telling me I don't know either as I don't even know who *they* are!' By now I was very annoyed and said to Tony, 'Just forget it. Maybe somewhere way back in the past you once told me something about that incident when you were a young boy and I remembered it.'

I knew that was not true, but by now I was well and truly fed up with the questions Tony was asking and eager to return to work. I knew I hadn't convinced him, but he started up the car and took me back to work. I made my apologies to the girl for being late. She smiled, saying it was all right with her. With that, she picked up her bag and said she would see me later. I was glad to be on my own and, as we were seldom as busy in the afternoons as the mornings, it gave me time to think over what I had seen by the river. It scared me.

For a split second I thought of the pills. Coming off them after all these years was hard, but could it be they had caused me damage to my mind? When my colleague came back after her lunch hour I decided to try to put it all at the back of my mind and get on with my work, hoping that nothing like it would happen again.

Tony picked me up from work that evening as usual and nothing was mentioned about it, which I was glad about. We went round to visit Mum that evening to see her and the girls, staying for an hour. When we got home I prepared all that I needed for work the next day, then sat down to watch television for the rest of the evening. I had only been watching television for about half an hour when, suddenly, the feeling I had had the previous day returned. I shivered and Tony must have noticed for he said, 'Are you feeling all right, love?'

'Yes, I'm fine,' I said, and he continued to watch the television.

Just then there was a knock at the front door. Tony got

up to see who it was. I turned the television sound down for I was intrigued to know who it was at that time of night. I could hear a man's voice talking to Tony but couldn't make out what was being said. Tony popped his head round the door and said, 'It's all right. I've left my car lights on, that's all,' and with that I heard the front door shut.

I got up to turn the sound up when suddenly I heard a voice call my name. I knew it wasn't Tony, for he was out in the street turning his lights off, and yet I heard someone call 'Ann' quite distinctly.

Good God, Ann, I thought to myself, you *are* going round the bend! and I turned the television up quite loud. I heard the front door open and Tony walked in asking what had happened on the television; there was a film we were watching, so I told Tony he hadn't missed much and we continued to watch it.

Suddenly, I heard the voice call, 'Ann' again. This time I nearly fell out of the chair and it frightened me for I heard it so clearly. Who the hell was it? I knew it wasn't Tony as it wasn't his voice and he was sitting quietly watching the television. My concentration went right off the film but I knew Tony was enjoying it so I decided that after it finished I would tell him. But by that time I had heard nothing else so I changed my mind and decided not to tell him after all. Perhaps it *was* my imagination after all?

That night and the following day everything was as normal so once more I tried to put it all behind me. That is, until we had settled down for the evening in front of the television when I heard the same voice again. That's it, I thought, I'm not going mad, I can hear it, and with that I got up and turned the television off. Tony looked shocked and asked what the matter was, so I explained everything that had happened.

'I don't know what the hell's going on but I know I can hear someone talking to me,' I told Tony. 'And I know it's not the drugs.'

'Why do you say it isn't the drugs?' asked Tony.

'Well, if I told anyone else I was hearing voices they

would obviously think it was the drugs that were the cause of it,' I said.

'Don't be silly,' he said. 'You only take four a day and if you were going to experience something like this you would have done so years ago when you were really ill and taking a large quantity of them.'

'Well, besides that, I would really like to know what's going on. I know it's no big deal but it frightens me a bit because I don't understand and I don't know who the voice belongs to. I only know I can hear it clearly.'

'What are the exact words that are being said?' he asked.

'I told you,' I said impatiently, 'just "Ann," nothing else, and there's this feeling I have that something or someone is around me when the name is spoken.'

'And nothing else?'

'No.'

'Why don't you ask whoever it is speaking what they want?' he suggested.

He had been interested in the subject of spiritualism for years, so I trusted him. I felt an idiot for I didn't know who or what I was speaking to, but to my utter astonishment, I heard the voice speak again. This time it said, 'Hello, Ann.'

I turned to look at Tony and said, 'It's no good. All I'm getting is "Hello, Ann".'

I was somewhat uptight with whoever the voice belonged to and wished it would just go away and said so to Tony.

'OK, then,' he said. 'Let's both try to forget it and maybe it won't come back any more. I can see it's worrying you.'

'Only because I don't understand,' I replied. 'I can honestly say I don't feel anything will harm me, but it's something that's never happened before and that's what's worrying me.' I paused for a moment and said, 'Tony, you don't think I'm cracking up, do you?'

Tony smiled and put his arm around me. 'Come on, love, let's wait and see if anything else happens,' and with that we went up to bed.

As I lay in my bed I hoped I had heard the voice for the last time. I put the pillow over my head, my old habit of a lifetime, and went to sleep. I could only have been asleep for a couple of hours when, I woke up with a start. I could distinctly hear people talking. The words were very jumbled, not easy to make out. I sat bolt upright and looked across at Tony, who was fast asleep. The pillow that had been over my head was missing and in a fit of panic I leant out of bed to see if it had fallen down by the side, but I couldn't feel it so I got out of bed to see where it had gone to. I looked under the bed and felt all around the bed itself, even under the eiderdown. It was nowhere to be seen. Suddenly I looked up at the pulled curtains, but why I didn't know. However, to my amusement, I saw the outline of the pillow behind them. I was absolutely flabbergasted and wondered how the hell it got there!

The voices that had woken me up were now getting faint and I grabbed my pillow from behind the curtain and got into bed quickly, pulling it tightly over my ears. For a little while I was too frightened to go to sleep and was hesitant as to whether I should wake Tony or not. I decided against it as I thought if I kept on about it too much Tony would begin to think I was seriously ill or something.

Despite the fact I had promised myself I would not think of it, I found it very difficult not to. At lunchtime Tony picked me up for our usual drive.

As the day went by I heard nothing more of the voices, which pleased me. I was beginning to feel much more relaxed and I hoped I had beaten it, whatever it was. What gave me the most satisfaction was that, during the whole of this odd occurrence, not once had I turned to the pills. I had come this far and my intake was still only four daily.

That evening, when we came home after visiting Mum and the girls, I prayed I wouldn't hear any more voices and made up my mind to tell Tony about the pillow incident. It made me nervous just thinking about it. I needed his support in case it happened again. I explained what had happened the previous night and looked at his face. I so needed him to believe me, but would he? It certainly sounded far-fetched.

Thankfully, he did believe me and I was so relieved.

'You don't think it is my coming off the pills that's doing it, do you?'

'Why should you think that?' he said, obviously surprised. 'You've never experienced anything like this before, so there's no reason to think it's them now.'

'I know that,' I said. 'But what is worrying me is that I don't know the reason for it all.'

'I don't think it is them,' said Tony. 'But I think I can come up with the answer. I think the spirit world is trying to make contact with you. In fact, since you started telling me about the voice saying "Ann", I was sure it was a spirit and I still think it is.'

I still wasn't convinced that what Tony was saying was true. Why should they want to contact me?

'Let's forget it,' I said. 'Perhaps I won't have any more contact. After all, I heard nothing this evening and I was hearing the voice around this time last night and the night before.'

By the time I got to bed that night I'd still heard nothing more, which made me feel much better. However, at the back of my mind I felt it wouldn't be the last of it. It wasn't that I feared the voice, but it unnerved me and I certainly didn't want a repeat performance of the previous night.

I had never been a good sleeper and it took some time for me to get off to sleep. Eventually, when sleep fell upon me, it seemed to me as if I had only been asleep a couple of minutes before, once again, I was woken up. This time when I heard talking the pillow was still in its rightful position over my head. Half-asleep, I wondered if I was dreaming and turned over, pulling the pillow more tightly over my ears. Sleep came across me once more until, yet again, I heard the voices, only this time they were a lot louder. No matter what I did with the pillow it made no difference, and so I decided to put both my pillows over my head, hoping they would block everything out. Instead the voices got even louder. I realised I was wasting my time trying to ignore them so I decided to listen to what they were trying to tell me. I took both the pillows away from my head, put my hands behind my head and just lay there. I could tell it was early morning because the light was coming through the windows. I looked at the clock for confirmation. Good God, I thought, it's only five o'clock! I was tired as I hadn't managed to go to sleep until the early hours, and had then woken up at this unearthly hour. There was no 'Hello, Ann,' this time but instead the voices seemed to be talking amongst themselves. How I knew it I don't know, but I did know there was more than one person speaking, and as much as I persevered I could not figure out what they were talking about. Whoever *they* were, *they* were keeping me awake and by now I was getting not only fed up with it but upset as well. Coming off the pills had affected my sleep. I had come to terms with that as I so desperately wanted to come off the drugs, but now I was being woken up early by voices which I didn't understand and that was difficult to cope with. I tried to remember what Tony had said the previous night about spirits wanting to get in touch with me and I thought, Well, if this is the way they were trying then I didn't want to know.

I put my hands over my ears and said out loud, 'Please, please, go away, whoever you are, please.'

But they didn't appear to listen to what I was saying, and continued talking. I had to get out of bed as they were driving me crazy when, suddenly, Tony woke up.

'What's the time, Ann?' he asked.

I looked at the clock. It was now gone six and I told him. Tony could tell by my face that all was not well and asked me what the matter was.

'Nothing,' I replied, trying my best to conceal my true feelings.

I went downstairs and turned on the electric fire. I sat down beside it with tears rolling down my face. The voices were still carrying on talking. I just didn't know what to do as it was obvious they were taking no notice of me. I hadn't been downstairs more than five minutes when Tony came into the living room. 'What the hell is the matter?' he demanded.

'They won't stop talking.'

'You mean the voices?'

'Yes, of course I mean the voices,' I snapped.

'All right, calm down, Ann,' Tony said, speaking more quietly. Although he knew what I was talking about in a sense, I knew he didn't fully understand, as he had never heard spirit himself or seen spirit. He sat down beside me and said, 'Come on, love, I'll make you a nice cup of tea. Perhaps if we talk about it or whatever, it might help.'

But in fact we were both perfectly helpless, neither of us knowing what to do. Tony made the tea and I sat there wiping away the tears and blowing my nose. I felt so vulnerable as I knew no one else, including Tony, could hear the voices. I was well aware Tony believed me implicitly and I tried to explain everything I was experiencing, but I was none the less feeling out on a limb.

When he came in with the tea he asked if I was feeling any better.

'Well,' I said, 'the voices seem to have gone.' I moved my head from side to side, trying to listen, but they had gone and I was relieved. I looked back at Tony and smiled.

'Yes, love, they've gone,' I repeated.

'Oh, I'm glad about that,' said Tony. 'Was it that bad?' he asked as if he almost daren't, or as if he didn't really want to know the answer.

'To be quite honest,' I said, 'they were driving me up the wall. I've been awake since five o'clock and up until now they haven't stopped.'

'I think it's time we had a bit of help on this,' said Tony.

A bit, I thought!

'We need all the help we can get!' I said. 'But how?' I asked.

'Well, I thought of Derek Markwell the other night when you were first hearing voices. It's time we gave him a ring, I think, don't you?'

Derek is a medium and a very good one at that. He had been a friend of ours for years and we knew he had a good reputation so we waited until a reasonable hour and phoned him. Unfortunately, he couldn't see us for a week, so as Tony put the phone down he said, 'Let's hope things will quieten down for a while. There is no one else I can ask.'

I tried to put things into perspective. 'Come on, let's go out for the day and try to take our minds off it.'

It was Sunday and there was no reason for us to sit around all day moping.

'Where do you want to go?' asked Tony.

'I don't care,' I replied. 'As long as I get out for a while.'

I must admit the day was a very peaceful one and I thoroughly enjoyed it. We managed to put our troubles to the back of our minds, we didn't get back till late and I even slept well that night. I heard no voices at all and the following morning I got up feeling wonderfully refreshed. As far as I am concerned there is nothing like a good night's sleep to put me in a good mood.

Chapter 11

The girl I worked with had Mondays as her day off. It was a quiet day as far as the workload went, thank goodness. After only an hour I had finished all the paperwork and was ready to serve the public. I was still feeling good after the happy day out followed by a good night's sleep. Today I felt like smiling.

As usual, Tony and I had our packed lunch by the river, but this time I kept chatting. Everything went well and, after our hour was up, Tony took me back to work.

I wasn't at all busy that afternoon so in between serving the customers I was able to sit and read a book. There was a stool near my chair where the other girl worked. I looked across at the stool, wishing she was there. I had become completely engrossed in the book, when all of a sudden I felt very cold. The weather was warm and sunny. I shuddered and shivered and tried to concentrate harder on my book, draping my cardigan round my shoulders. As I did so, a customer came up so I put my book down and served him, after which I tried to return to my book. But my thoughts were far from the story I was reading as I actually felt something or someone around me. I turned away from the window where I was sitting to look behind me. What it was I was expecting to see I don't know, but I had to look all the same. I knew nobody could have come into the office as I had the key, but at the same time, although I couldn't see anyone, I was convinced someone was there.

Good God, Ann, pull yourself together, I thought to myself and made an attempt to read my book once more. It was almost as if I was waiting for something to appear before my eyes, and as it happened I didn't have too long to wait. For suddenly, from out of nowhere, there was a shadow of a person. I couldn't see who it was, but nevertheless, there, in the corner of my office, the shadow stood. I stared at it, then looked back at the window. I knew I had seen it just as I knew I had heard the voices. I looked at my watch to see if it was time for Tony to come and pick me up. In a way I had accepted the voices to a certain extent, but to see a shadow and accept it, well, that was different. For some reason I didn't feel frightened or bothered by the shadow as I did with the voices. I felt secure in its presence. I decided to take a second look but this time the shadow had gone and in a way I felt sad. Whoever it was, I didn't want them to think I didn't like them.

I sat for a while, thinking over what was going on around me when I heard a voice say, 'Are you ready?'

This snapped me out of my thoughts and, seeing it was Tony, I said, 'Sorry, love, can you hang on for ten minutes?'

As a rule I would have had everything done by now and would be ready when he came for me, so he looked surprised when I asked him to wait. Soon, however, we were on our way home. We popped in to see Mum and the girls for an hour and then went on home. I told Tony about the shadow, but this time I didn't put any importance on what I had seen and it was almost as if I had accepted all of it without question or doubt, and Tony noticed this and remarked on it. He said, 'It is as if you have accepted what I said about spirit getting in touch with you, after all.'

'Yes, I have. Why, I don't really know, but yes, I think I agree with you now, although I don't pretend to understand any of it.'

'I'm sure you will in time.'

'I hope you're right,' I said, 'but if this talking continues I don't want any of it, I just can't cope if it means I have to lose my sleep at night.'

'I understand,' he said.

I had a question to put to him. 'If they are trying to get in touch with me, why is it me they want and not you?'

I had to ask this because for years Tony had always been interested in spiritualism, whereas I had only ever gone to a clairvoyant to tell me my future, and the spirit world in general had never appealed to me. There was only probably that one positive visit to a spiritualist Church.

'In my opinion,' Tony said, 'you should feel privileged and honoured that they have chosen you to speak to. I would love to be in contact with them, you don't know how fortunate you are.'

'Sorry, love,' I said, thinking I might have touched a nerve. 'It's just that it is all new to me and, although we're not perfect, I would have thought they would have picked someone better than me, especially with my past.'

'Ann,' said Tony in his stern voice, 'Stop knocking yourself. You were just ill and now you are getting better and that's all that matters.'

'That's all well and good, but if they keep me awake tonight then I don't want to know.'

Tony nodded in agreement and as I got ready for bed downstairs I felt the same coldness I had experienced at work that day. Once again I was aware someone was around me and whoever it might be I didn't want to scare them away, so I continued to get ready for bed. Tony was upstairs and in a way I was glad, for I sensed the spirit was pleased I was on my own. I sat down on the armchair in my night clothes and I asked who it was. There was no reply, which was what I had half-expected and I'm not sure why, but I had a lovely feeling of security about me and I knew I had nothing to fear.

When I got into bed I told Tony what had happened. He turned the bedside light out and said, 'I hope you have a good night,' and with that we both settled down to go to sleep. I heard him snoring within minutes of shutting his eyes. It wasn't long before I was asleep too.

Once again, after a couple of hours' sleep, I was woken up by the sound of voices, stronger and clearer than before. By morning I was shattered but I knew I had to go to work.

Tony telephoned Derek and told him that things had gone from bad to worse. Derek said he would be able to pop over to see me that morning.

'What about my job?' I asked Tony when he told me Derek was coming over.

'Don't worry,' he said. 'I'll pop down and see the girl you work with to tell her you are not very well,' and with that he went out.

I felt very nervous as Derek had not told us exactly what time he would come over and I didn't want to be on my own when he arrived. I phoned Mum to tell her I'd be round as usual that evening. I hadn't told her anything about what had been happening to me of late. I felt I didn't really know enough about it myself.

As I put the phone down I said out loud, 'Where the hell are you, Tony?'

He had been gone a good half an hour. Just then I heard a car pull up and, looking out of the window, I saw it was Tony. I gave a huge sigh of relief and opened the door for him. Not long after, Derek arrived with his wife. He said he knew exactly what to do. He told me he would have to perform an exorcism. He would start by saying the Lord's Prayer and call upon his guides to help me. He would need two glasses from which he would pour water from one to the other.

He carried out this procedure in every room and then once over my head. I understood nothing, but I trusted Derek completely and put myself in his hands. Everything seemed fine after he left but I didn't know what to expect or how I was supposed to feel. All I wanted was some peace of mind.

Tony could only have the morning off so he went back to work at lunchtime. I knew Mum and the children would be out so I decided to sit and have a quiet afternoon. I felt much more relaxed and confident since Derek had been so I lay on the settee, reading.

After a little while the phone rang. It was Tony checking to see if I was all right. I assured him I was well and went back to reading. Not long afterwards, I had that same feeling of being watched, that cold sensation coming over me. I slowly took my eyes away from the book and looked towards the kitchen door. The door itself was shut and between the wall and the door I could see a shadow. This time it was a bit clearer and I could see the outline. It was the outline of a Red Indian. I just sat still, staring at it. I didn't feel at all threatened, or frightened by it. My first thoughts were, Where the hell did he come from? and I wished could see him more clearly.

I don't know how long I stared but I do know I couldn't take my eyes away from him. Then, suddenly, as quickly as he appeared, he just vanished.

I sat still for a long time that afternoon, thinking about all the events of the past week. I had now fully accepted that I was in communication with the spirit world but the question was, why me? I had always been under the impression from the time I had started seeing mediums that they called upon good people, some of them even holy, and I certainly wasn't that. I began to think about what would happen this coming night. I still trusted Derek, but obviously the spirit had taken no notice. Tony came home early.

'Are you going round to your Mum's?' he said.

'Of course.'

'Well, I only asked, seeing you weren't well this morning.'

'No, I'm OK, love,' I said, and I told him all about what happened that afternoon. By the time I got back from Mum's I was eager to get to bed for I was absolutely shattered. I was in tears the following morning, for in the night the voices still kept me awake.

Tony rang Derek again, and this time he asked us if we would go to his house. Could we make it that evening? Tony went to my place of work to explain that I was still unwell and would not be in for the rest of the week. He went off to work after that and I went back to bed. For some unknown reason I knew I could get a couple of hours' sleep without any interruption. When I got up at lunchtime I felt a lot better, but I had made up my mind I didn't want to know the spirit world or anything to do with it whatsoever. I had to trust in Derek and I hoped that tonight he would be more successful.

I had just made myself a cup of tea and sat down when I saw the shadow. It was the Red Indian again.

'Please go away, whoever you are,' I said, and then turned away to look out of the window. I thought that if I simply ignored him he might take the hint and just go.

Just then I plainly heard the words, 'DON'T GO.' I turned away from the window to see if he was still standing there, but he had gone. Oh, well, I thought, at least he took notice of what I asked.

I had a few things to do before we went to Derek's. I phoned Mum to tell her I was going out, making up some excuse as I still didn't really want to tell her until it was all over.

As I put the phone down I heard, '*Don't go,*' this time louder. I looked around the room to see if the Indian had turned up again, but I couldn't see him.

'Don't go where?' I asked. I suddenly thought, thank God no one can see me! Here I am talking to thin air! But I could feel his presence in the room. On previous occasions I had only felt a shiver and then seen a shadow, this time I was well aware he was standing near me even though I couldn't see him at all.

'Don't go where?' I asked again.

'Man,' came back the reply.

At least I was getting some response, but I didn't know what it meant. Then it dawned on me. The only man I was going to see was Derek, but surely he wasn't telling me not to see him? Derek had worked for the spirit world for years and this Indian was a spirit, so why should he advise me not to go?

I knew I needed some form of help, so I told the Indian this was my only hope of getting some peace. By this time it was almost as if I had known the Indian for years.

Suddenly, everything went quiet and I knew his presence was no longer in the room with me. I sat back feeling very strange, for I had been talking to a spirit I knew nothing about and yet it had happened so naturally.

I had been sitting quietly for a while trying to digest what had happened when I heard the front door. I shot out of the armchair, realising I'd forgotten all about the time. I was still in my dressing gown when I opened the door sheepishly to Tony.

'Hello, love,' he said. 'How are you feeling now?'

'Well, I'm fine. Actually I've got something to tell you,' I told him all about the afternoon's experience. 'I'll leave you to think about it,' and I dashed upstairs to get ready to go to Derek's.

When I came downstairs Tony asked me why I hadn't phoned him at work to tell him what had been happening.

'Well, it didn't really bother me that much and I certainly didn't feel frightened by the spirit's presence. In fact, I felt quite happy with him,' I admitted.

'But what about being disturbed in the night?' Tony asked.

'Well, that I certainly don't want so I really do want Derek to remove it all, if at all possible.' We got our coats and left for Derek's house.

On our way there I was thinking about how tired I was feeling and how I would be glad when it was bedtime, but then I started thinking about the voices in my head. Although I was tired I was apprehensive about going to sleep in the knowledge that I would more than likely be woken up. I just hoped Derek would be able to help and I told Tony so. He said, 'Derek is a good medium, Ann, so I'm sure he'll be able to help. I know last time wasn't successful but maybe you'll have to see him again for him to get rid of them.'

We were not far from Derek's house now, when all of a sudden I felt the spirit was back.

'Tony, he's here,' I whispered.

'You what?'

'The Indian. He's here!'

'What's he want?'

'I don't know, do I!'

Tony tried to act calmly, telling me not to worry, we would soon be at Derek's house. But as I sat there I was feeling nervous for, although I had accepted the Red Indian being with me earlier that afternoon, he hadn't been as close to me. Now, his presence was almost overwhelming and I could sense he was angry. What he could possibly be angry about? Derek wouldn't hurt me, I trusted him. Just then, the car came to a halt.

'Here we are,' said Tony.

Thank goodness, I thought, maybe I can get something sorted out, but at the same time I was feeling sorry for the Indian, and, just as my emotions changed, so the answer suddenly came to me. What Derek was doing for me was taking the spirits away from me and that was the reason the Indian didn't want me here. I spoke, hoping he would understand. 'I'm sorry, but all of this is making me ill. I've just got to see Derek.' Tony asked me if I was all right as he rang the front door bell of Derek's house.

'Yes, I'm fine.' The Indian was still with me even as Derek greeted us and showed us into his living room.

As I sat down I tried to ignore the Indian, but it was very difficult.

Just then, without any warning, I turned to Derek, bringing my hand clutched across my chest and said, 'The Indian greets you.'

It all happened so quickly that I felt embarrassed. Derek is one of the very best mediums. It made me feel a bit of a fool.

'Sorry about that, Derek,' I said, 'but there is this Indian around me.'

'Don't worry,' replied Derek, 'I understand. The Indian was greeting me as a friend but in anger.'

I sat back for a moment in amazement. How did Derek know he was angry?

'I have an Indian guide so I'm aware of the signs,' explained Derek. 'And I can assure you he is definitely not pleased with me.'

I told Derek what had happened over the past couple of days and explained I didn't mind if it happened during the day, but I couldn't cope with not sleeping at night-time. Derek understood and explained that, if it was meant for me to have spirit with me, then more than likely he wouldn't be able to help me. I accepted what he said and Derek performed another exorcism, but whilst he was carrying it out the Indian came in stronger than ever, and he wasn't happy. As I sat waiting for Derek to finish, I knew there was absolutely no way I was going to get rid of this spirit. Derek confirmed this. 'All we can hope for, Ann, is that tonight it might calm them down a bit, but I can't remove the spirit from you.'

I thanked him for trying and asked, 'I would like to know if it's possible to tell me who the Indian is.'

'Yes, he's your guide.'

I had heard mediums talk about their guides before and knew they were there for protection, but that was about all. 'Is this Indian here to protect me, Derek?'

'Yes, he is.'

As we left Derek's house all the thoughts I had had about the spirit world upsetting my sleep left me. Instead, I was concentrating on the Red Indian. Somehow it made me feel good that someone was protecting me.

The Indian didn't come back that evening but in a way I was hoping he wouldn't stay away for ever. As much as I was feeling ill from lack of sleep, I had felt so at ease in the Indian's presence and I hoped it hadn't been the last time I would see him.

As I turned over to try to sleep, I spoke to the spirit voices. 'Please don't keep me awake tonight. Please go away,' and as I said those words my eyes shut. Suddenly, I saw a large window and behind that window there were many faces. I could see them clearly, but what struck me was how miserable they looked. I somehow sensed it was because of what I had just said. As I looked back at them I felt riddled with guilt, so I felt I needed to explain myself. 'Look,' I said, 'I don't mind talking to you, but I can't go on without sleep. If you understand what I'm saying to you why don't you all try talking to me during the daytime, rather than during the night?'

All of a sudden their expressions changed from sad to happy. I wondered why I hadn't tried talking directly to them before, but anyway I hoped it would work and I drifted off to sleep. I *was* woken up again but the voices were much quieter and, although I was woken up twice, I found it wasn't so difficult to get back to sleep again.

That morning I told Tony what I had said to them before I went to sleep and that seemed to have quietened them down a little.

'Well,' said Tony, looking relieved, 'let's see how it goes in the next couple of days. I'm so glad you didn't have too bad a night.'

I smiled at him for I was glad of his support. Anyone else would have surely thought I was potty.

In the evening Tony asked me how things had been that day. I told him I had had no vision of the Indian.

'You sound a bit disappointed,' he said.

'Yes, I am in a way,' I replied. 'I rather liked his presence.'

The next day Mum and I went shopping and when we got back I settled down to a quiet afternoon at home. Tony put a film on for us both to sit and watch. All of a sudden I felt the Indian's presence. As I looked up I could see his shadowy form, but this time it was a little clearer. I saw he had his arms folded and I was very pleased to see him and told him so.

Tony noticed my attention had wandered from watching the film and asked me what the matter was.

'He's back!' I said excitedly.

'You mean the Indian?'

'Yes.' Tony got up to turn the video off, asking me if the Indian was saying anything.

'No, he's just standing there.'

Tony sat back down. 'Why don't you ask him who he is or something?'

'Like what?' I asked. 'As far as I'm concerned he's my guide.'

'Well, try asking him anything, just to see what he says.'

Anything to keep the peace, I thought, so I looked back to where the Indian was standing. He just stood there looking back at me.

'Aren't you going to say anything?' I said.

There was no reply, so I said to Tony, 'He's not saying anything.'

'We might as well finish the film then,' said Tony, and got up to put the film back on. I looked back at the Indian but he had gone, although I sensed his presence, and as I watched the television I heard the same voice I had heard the other day which said, 'Hello Ann.' I knew it was a man's voice, but it didn't belong to the Indian. I asked Tony to turn off the television, as, for some unknown reason, I knew I was about to have a conversation with this spirit. Tony was wondering what on earth was happening so I said, 'Sorry, love, it's just that someone's here and I'm sure he's going to say something.'

'Who's here? The Indian?' asked Tony.

'No, all I know is it's a man's voice.'

Tony sat there dumbfounded. Just then, the man whose voice it was stood in front of me. I could see him vividly. He was smoking a pipe, as solid a human being as you or I.

Tony said, 'Well, tell me what's happening to put me out of my misery.'

The man told me to describe him to Tony. I told Tony how he was dressed, and that he was smoking a pipe.

Tony looked flabbergasted and asked me to describe the man again, as if he hadn't believed what he had heard the first time. After I had finished Tony got up. 'I won't be a minute,' he said, and with that he rushed upstairs.

The man standing in front of me smiled and said, 'I like you.'

I felt both bemused and embarrassed by his kind compliment. 'Why thank you,' I said, wondering what the hell to say next! I heard Tony running downstairs. As he entered the room I could see he was carrying something.

'Look at this and tell me who it is,' he said.

It was a photograph of the man who was standing in front of me. I told Tony.

'He's my Dad.' He looked and sounded both shocked and stunned.

'I'm sorry, love,' I said, 'I didn't realise it was him.'

'No, it's all right,' he said. 'Go on, please. It's the first time I've ever had contact from him.'

Tony's father had died before I met Tony and I had never really asked about him.

I looked at Tony's father and said to him, 'I'm sorry, but I don't remember ever having seen a photograph of you before.'

He said, 'Tell Tony about the fish,' and he held up a barbel fish. He added, 'Remember to say its name, barbel. He'll know what I mean.'

'He's on about a fish,' I said to Tony. 'It looks big to me. It's a barbel.'

Tony looked amazed. 'How did you know that?' he asked with staring eyes.

'Your Dad just told me.'

'That's something you couldn't have known about, Ann.' He explained to me it was the biggest fish his Dad had ever caught and Tony was with him the day he caught it!

'That's amazing,' he said. 'It's not that I didn't believe you, but this is extraordinary.'

His very own father was here, in the same room as us, giving his son concrete evidence of life after death. I was thrilled for Tony for I knew how much it meant to him to have communication from his father.

Tony's father wasn't the only visitor that weekend. It was almost as if a whole new spirit world had opened up for me. I could see and hear all of them as clearly now. Many spirit people communicated, many of them family, including Tony's Uncle Bob, who was a lovely man.

Chapter 12

It didn't take very long for me to settle down with the spirit world and the Red Indian was now always present, but in the shadows. Whoever I spoke to from the spirit world I was aware that the Indian was with me too, and I was happy to know he was there. I don't know why, but I felt a bond between us and although I loved the company of the spirit people it was different with the Indian.

Within two or three months I was able to see and hear the spirit people as perfectly as the living. So far only Tony knew what was going on, I still hadn't said a word to Mum, but I knew I would have to say something sooner or later. There were times when I was saying things without really being aware of what I was saying in front of Tony, and I was worried I would do the same with Mum. So one night I decided to tell her all about it. When I arrived she was sitting in the living room watching television with Joyce. Karen was upstairs getting ready to go out.

'Mum, can I have a word with you on your own?' I asked.

'Yes, of course you can,' she said as she got up to go into the kitchen. She asked if anything was wrong.

'No, I said,' 'I just want to have a little chat, that's all.'

I could tell by the expression on her face that she thought it was to do with the pills, so I put her mind at rest. 'I'm fine, really, and before you start worrying it's nothing to do with the pills.'

She sighed with relief and smiled, then walked towards the cooker to put the kettle on. As I sat down waiting for her to make the tea, I wondered what her reaction would be. I truly wanted her to believe me. She had some idea about spirit for I had told her about the times I had been to see a medium, but her attitude had always been 'When you're dead, you're dead.' Sometimes she said, 'Do you really believe in all that rubbish?' So I knew what I was up against.

Mum came over to sit down with the tea. 'Well, what's it all about, then?' she asked.

I took a deep breath and told her all about the events of the past months, including Tony's father and his Uncle Bob and all the other spirit people, but most of all about the Red Indian.

Saying nothing, she just sipped her tea.

'Aren't you going to say anything, then?'

'Well, you know my opinion on that subject,' she replied. 'I don't really believe in all that, but on the other hand that doesn't mean I don't believe you.'

Thank God for that, I thought.

'I've never heard you say anything like this before,' she said, 'so I can't see why you should make it all up now.'

The one thing about my mother, she would always come straight to the point and speak her mind.

'The thing is, Ann, are you happy being able to talk to whoever it is you talk to?'

I laughed to myself for I knew she wouldn't say 'spirit'.

'Yes, Mum, I am. 'I can't put into words how much happier I am feeling than I have been for a long time.'

'Then that's all that counts, love. And have you thought that if you are that happy you might not need the pills any more?'

I sat and stared at her. I hadn't really thought about the pills very much lately. I was still on my four a day, but I must admit that since meeting the spirit world the pills weren't paramount in my life. Mum had come up with a question, which hadn't crossed my mind. 'Well let's hope so, Mum, but that would be a miracle in itself.'

It was no secret that if Mum had one wish it would be for me to be completely cured of drugs, and I could see a tiny glimmer of hope in her eyes. When I was back home that evening, I was thinking about the Indian. So far he had been in the shadows for a considerable time and I just wished he would show himself to me properly. I had a feeling he would

turn up soon. In fact I had to wait until the following week
It happened one evening when I was sitting, reading a book.
Tony was upstairs doing some studying when the presence of
the Indian felt very strong indeed. Taking my eyes off the book
I looked down and noticed a pair of feet on the floor in front
of me. On the feet were a pair of gaily-coloured moccasins.
Very cautiously I looked straight ahead and there stood the
Red Indian as solid and as normal as any human being on
earth. My book dropped out of my hands. I sat there in awe
of this spirit, and as I cast my eyes over him I could see he
had such clear, blue eyes. He was a good six feet tall and
majestic in his stance. Around his head was a band holding
his hair off his face and on each side of his face his hair was
plaited in brown leather strips. I could see he had a feather
hanging loosely down one of his shoulders and another plait
down the back of his hair with a feather plaited in between.
The feather was a brilliant white.

I knew the feather had some significance, but I wasn't
sure exactly what it was. I looked back at the eyes again
and somehow I knew they were smiling at me. There were
lines around his eyes and I could tell he had somehow earned
them in some way or another. He had more lines around his
mouth and just then he started to smile. His lips parted and
he started to laugh. I expect it was because of the expression
on my face at the time! His beautiful teeth were brilliant white
and gleaming. He suddenly stopped laughing but his smile
didn't go away. Looking up at him I hoped he wouldn't go
and that he would always appear like this.

He was only about twenty-four years old but he looked
a bit older. I could tell by looking at his eyes that he had
had to grow up quickly but then again he had kept some of
his boyish charms. I started to look down past his face and
saw he had a thick neck, wide shoulders, and a very broad
chest, and as he breathed I could see the muscles rippling.
His waist was almost the same size as his hips, but a fraction
smaller, and he wore a loin cloth. His legs were strong-looking
and his skin was a beautiful bronze colour.

I thought to myself that I had seen many old cowboy and

Indian films and had I ever wished for a good looking Indian, then here was one right in front of me. He started laughing at me again as he stood there with his arms crossed. I noticed he had two armbands on, one was high up on one arm, the other near to his wrist on the other, and both brightly coloured.

I looked back at his neck to see he had a necklace, made of what looked like animal teeth.

Just then he stopped laughing again and unfolded his arms. He lifted one arm up behind him and pulled out an arrow. I hadn't noticed it before, but could now see he had a strap across his chest which held a small leather container on his back where he kept his arrows.

He took hold of the arrow and held it out in front of me. I could tell he was trying to say something to me and it then dawned on me why he had only said three words to me in the past. He had only a limited knowledge of English. It was obvious he was trying to tell me something important, don't ask me how I knew, but I could sense he had something to say.

I looked at the arrow he was holding, then looked back at him and said quietly 'What does it mean?'

His other hand moved towards the feather, the one which was hanging down, and he brought it forward, putting the arrow next to it. I looked at the arrow and the feather but still didn't have a clue what he was trying to tell me. He pointed to the feather with the arrow. I could think of was how bright the white of the feather looked, and in a way this seemed to be an important factor. It was the *white* colour of the feather which drew my attention most of all and I knew he was trying to tell me his name.

'*White* what?' I asked him once more, and again he produced both the feather and the arrow. At first I thought of White Feather or White Arrow and when he brought the arrow forward I knew it to be White Arrow.

'That's it,' I exclaimed. 'Your name is White Arrow!'

By the expression on his face I could tell I was right, and then he smiled at me.

'Hello, White Arrow,' I said, smiling back. 'It's nice to know your name at last and also to see you so clearly.'

He just nodded his head and smiled but said nothing.

I sat there feeling elated. For a moment I feared he might go away and never come back. I felt so close to him now that I really didn't want him to ever leave. I had been so terribly hurt in the past and I had promised myself nothing else would hurt me again. As I looked at the Indian I told him this and thought to myself, if only he could speak English. If only someone from the spirit world was around who could explain to him my feelings and anxieties, it would make it much easier to communicate with him.

I didn't have the chance to find out if the Indian knew what I was thinking and saying, for Tony came downstairs.

'How's the book?' he asked.

I had forgotten all about the book I had been reading by now and started to tell him I had seen the Indian properly just minutes ago and I knew the Indian's name. I didn't tell Tony I didn't want the Indian to go, for I had no wish to upset him. I thought it best not to say anything at this stage.

He was eager to hear all about the Indian, what he looked like and how I knew his name.

'It looks like it will be difficult for you to communicate with him,' said Tony.

'Yes, I know,' I replied. 'But I am hoping he'll learn to speak English as we go along. I'm just pleased I know his name now and in a way it is good that I had understood what he was trying to tell me without him having spoken at all.'

From that day on White Arrow was around most of the time, and each time he appeared he was always in a solid, large as life form. He was no longer just a shadow but as a normal human being and, no matter what, I found I now loved him. Tony was aware of all this and whenever White Arrow was around Tony knew somehow and I didn't have to tell him.

I can't explain fully, but I certainly did feel much happier when any of the spirit people were around me. I told Tony and I wondered if it upset him.

No, love,' he replied. 'I just hope they don't take you away from me, that's all.'

'Oh, come on, love,' I said. I walked towards him and put my arms around him. 'They are spirit, people from the next world who were once earthly beings, you are here and very much alive. Nothing can come between us, I promise.'

'Well, I'm not so sure,' he said, and walked away from me.

'What does that mean?' I said, following him out to the kitchen. 'Come on, you might as well tell me what's bugging you.'

'It's him, White Arrow,' he said, marching back into the living room.

'Oh, for God's sake, he's only a spirit.'

'Yes, I know he is. I'm sorry, but it's just that he seems to take all of your attention lately.'

'I'm sorry, love,' I said. 'This is all as new to me as it is to you and I suppose I have ranted on a lot about him and the spirit world, but I didn't mean to, it's just that you are the only one I can really talk to who understands me.'

Poor Tony looked so hurt. I didn't want to give up the spirit world or White Arrow, but if it was hurting him I would try to stop it all and I told him so.

'No, I don't want you to do that,' he replied. 'Just give me time to adjust to it all and I'm sure I'll find it all as intriguing as you do, and I think it's marvellous that you have the ability to communicate with them. But as much as it is new to you, it's also a lot for me to take in.'

I could sympathise with Tony and knew we would both have to learn to adjust to what was happening around us. One thing was evident to me now, and that was that our lives would never be the same again.

I found that in my daily life the spirit people would turn up at odd times but always White Arrow would be there, almost as if he was protecting me. I didn't mind and quite enjoyed the company. I also found whenever I was in the company of friends, that someone they once knew who had passed over would pop in to say hello. I would describe them and whoever they belonged to instantly recognised them. Early one evening when we had some friends round, we were chatting about what had been happening lately, and I was telling them about White Arrow, when he suddenly turned up at my side. Naturally, I told them he was here and one of my friends asked, 'Does he ever say anything?'

I explained that I understood his English must be rather limited, that he had only ever said three words to me.

Just then, White Arrow made me jump for he said, quite clearly, 'Big bird in sky,' and he pointed upwards.

I was absolutely taken aback, for he had been silent for so long and now he here was talking about a big bird in the sky!

Tony asked me what the matter was for he saw my attention had been taken away, so I told him that White Arrow had actually said something at long last. I repeated White Arrow's words and Tony reckoned he was talking about an aeroplane.

'Of course,' I agreed. 'It's got to be that.'

Tony said White Arrow wouldn't have known the word 'aeroplane' as they didn't have them in his day.

'Maybe I'm going on a journey by plane,' I said.

'Ask him then,' said one of my friends.

They were a couple we had known for some time who had always been interested in spiritualism, so it was lovely to be able to share the experience with them. I turned to White Arrow and asked him the question. He pointed to the woman and repeated the words, 'Big bird in sky.'

'It's for you,' I told her. 'It's you who will be going on a plane journey.'

I had a feeling something else was going to be said, don't ask me how, for White Arrow said nothing more, but I asked them all to be quiet for a moment. They all sat patiently. Just then, a teepee was in front of me. I could see it as clear as day and it was moving backwards and forwards. I sat there, staring at it, when suddenly I seemed to know what it all meant. I looked up at the couple and, without thinking, asked them if they were contemplating moving house. The strange thing is that the movement the teepee was making was very erratic, which made me think they weren't sure about the move being the right decision.

'Well,' said my friend, 'we are thinking about moving, but we haven't made our minds up what to do for the best yet.'

My reply was, 'Well, you are going to move, I can assure you,' and they both looked at me in amazement. I could tell they weren't quite convinced about what I had told them, but I didn't care.

'Is there anything else?' asked Tony.

I sat quietly for a moment, but there was no sound from White Arrow and I couldn't see anything. I was just about to give up when suddenly I saw a circle with a cross inside it. Once again, I sat bewildered, trying to figure it out. Slowly, the circle started to get darker. It had been a light colour when I first saw it but now it was quite dark. Within seconds of seeing it I knew what it meant. I don't know how, but looking back at the couple I asked them if anyone close to them had been very depressed lately. I felt there had been tears shed by this person and I told them so. They both looked at me surprised and said, 'Yes, we're both very worried about a member of our family who is ill. It has caused many tears all round.'

For some unknown reason I looked back at the circle and this time it was no longer dark, but the same light colour it was when I first saw it. I turned to my friends and smiled.

'They're going to be all right now.'

Just then, White Arrow brought the teepee in again and this time there was another one next to it, but it was a much smaller one. Once more I knew exactly what it meant, but before I could tell them I saw the circle again, this time by the side of the small teepee. The small teepee had told me that there was small child living in the house, and it was the child who was ill and who they were all worrying about. The circle was still a light colour and I knew instantly that the child would be well, and I passed this information on to them. They confirmed I was spot on. I was both pleased and puzzled at the same time, pleased because they accepted all that I told them and puzzled because it was amazing how I knew what the objects indicated. White Arrow then vanished and soon afterwards our visitors left.

As I lay in bed that night I thought about the messages and how they had been shown to me, when suddenly it dawned on me. I had known White Arrow couldn't speak much English so he was passing messages on to me in Indian signs. However, what surprised me most was that I knew without asking exactly what they meant and it was the first time White Arrow was actually communicating with me, and I was also pleased it was at a time when I could share it with friends and hopefully it helped them, too.

Chapter 13

Over the months that followed, most of White Arrow's communication with me was shown in Indian terms, but there were occasions when he tried to speak in English, but it was very broken English. The funny thing is that, whenever he was talking to me in this type of pidgin English, without me realising it, I was doing just the same. I was picking up his way of speaking. By now I had told Mum and the girls all about my spirit guide and the spirit people who I had communication with, and thankfully they accepted it fully.

Mum and the kids liked White Arrow's name. It got to the stage that wherever I went he would follow me, but it was very nice having him around and I got used to it. I believe the girls thought it was all a game at the beginning, for whenever I was at their house they would ask me where he was and what he was doing or saying.

My elder daughter Karen and I were still not as close as I would have liked, not like I was with my younger Joyce, and I hoped that now that I was feeling better than I had been for years it would somehow draw us together. But the damage was done and I had to accept it. The only thing I could wish for was that she wouldn't carry the hate she had for me all her life, like I had done with my father.

One day, when I was at Mum's house, Karen was sitting in the living room when she suddenly turned to me and asked me why the spirit world should choose somebody like me to communicate with. I was somewhat hurt by her question, but I told her I honestly didn't know why they chose me.

When I arrived home later that day I asked White Arrow if he could answer my daughter's question. Even though White Arrow's English was not very good, whatever words he used I easily understood. I heard the words, 'I need you, Little One.'

It was the first time White Arrow had referred to me as Little One and for a moment I was puzzled.

'You, Little One.'

'What a lovely name to call me,' I said, feeling very flattered and privileged. Then my mind immediately went back to what the nun had said to me the day Mum had come to collect me. What a strange coincidence, I thought, but it soon went out of my mind when White Arrow started to speak to me again.

'You must follow me,' he said.

'Where?'

'You must follow me,' he repeated.

'Do you mean follow you as in follow wherever you take me, or what?' I asked, not fully understanding what he meant.

'Speak,' he answered, and he pointed to his mouth. I knew then exactly what he meant. Whatever he said, I had to take notice and that's what he meant by following him.

'I do wish you would learn to speak English properly, White Arrow,' I said. It's difficult sometimes knowing what you mean straight away. So, let me get this right, you want me to take notice of what you say.'

'Yes.'

He went on to say, 'Daughter did not mean . . .', but before he could finish his sentence I butted in.

'But she didn't mean to be disrespectful about you, White Arrow,' I said.

I didn't want to hear what he had to say in case it was something I wouldn't like. I couldn't risk being hurt any more. I had put up a barrier around me which would let no one in.

'No, Little One,' said White Arrow. 'No barrier, please,' and he spoke in a soft voice.

'I know,' I replied, 'but I can't be hurt any more.'

I wished I knew what the bond was between myself and White Arrow and why he had chosen the name of Little One, but the bond was there and it was special. I looked at Tony, who was sleeping peacefully next to me, and everything suddenly seemed crystal clear.

White Arrow was standing by my side and as I looked at

him I said, 'Yes, I love you and maybe I understand why we are so close, but I love him, too,' and I looked over at Tony who was still fast asleep. As I looked at my husband Tony, I smiled to myself. Not everyone thought he was a good man, but to me he was and that was all that mattered, and I loved him dearly. I could see both of them so clearly, which was a weird and wonderful situation to find myself in, to say the least. Here I was, with a husband who was very much alive and well, and also I had a spirit man whom I shared my life with. I repeated I loved him but as much as I did, my love for Tony was greater. White Arrow accepted this and nodded. As I looked at both of them I wondered if maybe it wasn't such a good idea to tell Tony all this. He was convinced about the spirit world's existence and previous reincarnations, and if I was to tell him I believed I somehow knew White Arrow in a former life, he might well believe it. Whether he would like it or not remained to be seen. I looked up at White Arrow for his advice. He was shaking his head as if to say 'No' it wasn't the right time. There was something about the twinkle in White Arrow's eyes that told me he was full of mischief.

'White Arrow, if you say anything I'll kill you,' I said without thinking.

White Arrow laughed his head off and when I realised what I had said I saw the funny side of it, too. I couldn't kill him, even if I wanted to, for he was already dead!

'You can laugh,' I said to him, 'but I mean it, I'll tell him when I'm good and ready. Promise me you'll behave yourself!' and with that he vanished. I tried to put it all behind me but somehow I knew White Arrow wouldn't let it drop so I would just have to be on my guard with him. As I looked at Tony I thought, You poor thing, having to put up with a spirit like White Arrow!

Chapter 14

One Sunday afternoon, Tony was sitting reading the paper and I was watching the television relaxing when, suddenly, my mind seemed to go somewhere else. I found myself in a place far, far away from this country and I was no longer in my living room. I was crying . . .

I was crying so much that my mouth felt bone-dry, and my skin was hot and burned. The smoke was also burning me and my throat. There I was, a small baby, and yet I knew and could feel all that was happening around me, and it was amazing for one so young to have such a crystal clear picture of the whole scene. I knew I had been there for a time, maybe hours, or perhaps a whole day, and that the wagon was on its side. There were no horses, for I could clearly see the broken reins as if the horses had torn them apart as they fled in fear, and yet somehow I knew the Indians had taken them.

Suddenly there was an Indian on a horse in front of me. He was so gentle and as he picked me up the love in his eyes, the strength in his arms, made me stop crying. I felt safe with him but then, in a flash, I went back in time, to just before the burning smoke had enveloped me.

The wagons were rolling and I knew there were only about ten or twelve wagons around us. I was in the back of our wagon whilst my mother, brother and father were in the front. Father was driving the horses as my brother was next to him, fast asleep on my mother's lap. It was so hot that my mother had to keep wiping her face and neck with a scarf as the sweat was pouring from her body. It was still daylight but we were tired from all the travelling we had done all day. By now the dust and heat had got to us and Father looked very tired. I know my brother's name was John and as he lay blissfully sleeping across my mother's lap her long dark hair was pushed back, hanging down her back under her bonnet. She kept looking behind her to see if I was all right in the back of the wagon and then she would wipe Father's forehead.

Just then a man drew up on a horse at the side of our wagon to speak to my father. Soon we will settle for the night, but we must use as much of the daylight as possible. Father knew the number of miles we had to cover before the homeland was in sight. We wanted to reach it badly, but we had to rest at night.

Father was becoming more and more concerned about one of the wheels of our wagon. That night one of the other men helped him repair it. Father had a dark beard and looked much older than Mother, who was about twenty-six. My brother was about eight years old whilst I was about six months to a year. My mother was a pretty young woman, and every time my parents looked at each other I could see the deep love they had for each other.

Despite the fact that they were both hot and tired they did not exchange any cross words, but we were all very happy and looking forward to what was going to be a brand new beginning to the rest of our lives.

Dusk was falling by this time and I think Father must have been in charge, because once again the man on the horse appeared to speak with him to ask if he wanted the wagons to rest for a while or to carry on. Father looked at him and told him that the people were tired and weary and ready for a well-earned rest, so we would go forward just until we found a suitable place that would be safe. The man rode off to carry out his instructions.

My brother was waking now. Even at his age he seemed a man as he asked Father if he could help him with the reins. Father looked at him and smiled, then looked at Mother so proudly. He couldn't look round at me because of driving the wagon, but asked if I was all right. Mother smiled, 'She's fine,' and turned to pick me up and put me on her lap. By now my brother was sitting up next to Father, playing happily, whilst Father looked full of pride for here was his family, content in the knowledge that we were on our way to a new land. And he was also so proud to have a son who would carry on his name and proud of his daughter because she looked like his wife, the woman he loved so much. He leant across to stroke my hair and as he did so they smiled lovingly at each other.

Suddenly there was a cry from afar, yet I managed to recognise the voice – it belonged to the man on the horse and he was indicating to us that he had found a place to stop. It was now getting dark and Father was shouting to the wagon behind us that we were going to stop ahead to rest awhile, and the message was passed on in turn to all the other wagons. Gradually, the wagons formed a circle and slowly came to a halt. Father got down first and then helped Mother and, one by one, the rest of us. Mother went to the back of the wagon, taking us with her whilst Father untied the horses to give them a well-earned rest, and something to eat and drink. All the women started to get their pots and pans together to prepare food for their families. The men, in the meantime, were checking the wagons and horses for safety and started making fires. The children were running about, playing happily.

The air was stifling, it was hot with no breeze, yet the people were comforted with the thought of what tomorrow should bring forth. They were able to relax a after such a long day. The women chatted amongst themselves. Mother was moaning that her dress had been torn that day; after all, she did not have many to her name, but Father laughed and said that when we reached our new homeland she could make many.

After the fires had been lit, the horses tended to and the cooking was all done, everyone began to settle down beside one another by the fire and Mother put me between herself and Father, making sure the blankets were underneath me as the ground was still very hot from the day's brilliant sun. My brother was somewhere about, playing with the other children, my father keeping a watchful eye on him so he couldn't go too far away. If he did go out of my father's sight he got called back because this was dangerous country.

Father turned to Mother to say he must go and mend the wheel as it would not last another day, and with that he called to his friend and together they went back to the wagon. They were gone for about an hour or so and, when Father returned, he said to Mother, 'It was not as bad as I thought. I hope it will last to the end of the journey.'

'I do hope that it will not be too long now,' said Mother.

Father stroked her hair and replied, 'Wait till we get there and you'll see, you'll be so happy, I know the journey has been hard and trying.'

Mother laughed and said to him, 'It's all right, I'm not moaning, I just feel sorry for the children. It must be so hard for them.'

This time Father spoke very quietly to her, 'When we get there and settle down they will soon forget, don't worry,' and he gazed down at me.

It was almost as if he had forgotten all about me, but when he looked at me I could tell by looking in his eyes that he had not. I then turned to face my mother and held my arms outstretched so she picked me up, and as she cuddled me the love and the warmth she felt for me was all the proof I needed. I felt such deep, sincere love from her.

'I think the children should go to bed now,' said my father, 'and why don't you go, too? You look so tired.'

'Come on, John,' my mother shouted to my brother, and many of the other mothers were also calling their children to do the same. John came to her straight away.

'He is a good boy,' said my father.

Mother smiled and picked me up and started walking towards the wagon with John holding her hand, and myself with her other arm. She turned to say to Father, 'Good night, may God be with you.'

It had been agreed that Father would be on watch all night and that Mother would lead the wagons for half the following day so that Father could sleep. She had done it before and had learnt, as women of that time had to.

Mother put me behind the front seat of the wagon. It was now getting cold, so she wrapped me up well. John went to the back of the wagon – he knew where his bed was for he made it himself. Mother looked at him so proudly for he had never asked her how to make his bed and they looked at each other, their eyes telling the bond of love there was between them, and

Mother also feeling so proud of having a young son who was trying so hard to be a man. Very soon my brother was asleep and I knew my mother was not worried about him but was now looking at me and caressing me. As she sang to me with her soft voice, I remember her blue eyes and her gentle words. There I was, a blue-eyed, dark-haired baby with a healthy, well-fed body. A smiling, contented baby with no cares in the world because I was loved. At my tender age nothing mattered to me other than the knowledge that I was being loved and cared for. I did not know or understand that one year previously my parents had been through hard times because they wished for happiness for their children. As my mother looked at me I remember so vividly her dark hair falling across her face, her skin burnt by the sun and her slim figure. Her eyes were shiny and bright as if the excitement of thinking of tomorrow was too much to bear. As she bent forward her hair felt soft between my fingers as I played with it. The words of the lullaby she sang were of the love she had for me and, as my arms stretched out to her, I knew she wanted me to go off to sleep. I felt so contented that her wish came true and within seconds I was fast asleep.

The next thing I remember was Mother breast-feeding me. It was still dark yet, the early hours of the following morning, and I could just see the first glimpse of daylight. Mother was singing to me – I say singing, but it was more humming really because there were no words. I felt the silence and, as my mother was feeding me, I sensed she felt uneasy about something, that there was something not quite right. The silence was almost deafening for there was no sound about us at all – no birds, no insects, just as if the whole world had stopped still. Even at my young age I felt fear and the fear in my mother was growing, but I didn't know why. Just then, my brother seemed to be saying, 'Mother', but it did not seem the right word as he had difficulty in getting the word out properly. In my short life I had never seen fear as I was now seeing it on my mother's face. The memory I have of that look of hers is so vivid and yet it was probably over in seconds. Somehow it seemed to last for ever. The reason for my mother's expression was because between the open flaps at the back of our wagon stood an Indian with his bow and arrow aimed ready to fire. My brother had seen him first which was why he tried to call my mother to warn her, but he was so frightened he could not move fast enough. The Indian had not seen my brother but could only see Mother's back and did not realise she was breast-feeding her baby. The Indian couldn't see me in her arms at all and was unaware of my presence. My brother knew his mother was about to be killed so he moved forward and, although he was frightened of the outcome, it somehow didn't matter to him for he knew what the Indian's intentions were. As he tried to utter the word 'Mother' the arrow was released from the bow and within seconds was deep in my brother's back. He fell, almost to my mother's side, her little son who was a man at just eight years old. Mother screamed in terror and laid me to one side whilst she stretched out her arms, grabbing her son to cradle him in her arms, knowing all was lost. The Indian then climbed up into the wagon, seeing he had not killed the one he had intended to. Mother had a rifle which she always kept close by, as did all the folk in those days. She had never had to use a rifle before and had never wanted to and yet now she knew she had to and wanted to. She picked it up and shot him point-blank. Mother was shaking and the smell of the gun smoke was strong. The Indian lay in the wagon and a part of his body was on her son's feet. This revolted her so she pulled her son's body away from the Indian. The arrow had killed him outright.

Within seconds she heard gun-fire and screaming. She knew she had lost her son but I was still here safe and well, so her next concern was for me. Earlier that morning the men had hitched the wagons to the horses and fed them in order to make an early start before it was completely light. By now the horses were restless with all the noise. Besides her fear for my safety, Mother was worried about my father. She did not know if he was dead or alive. Just then the wagon went forward, but not as if we were on the move. With the jolt, Mother fell over backwards towards the back of the wagon. In fear she grabbed me, but once again fell as the wagon jerked forward, making her fall with me in her arms, on top of the dead Indian and her dead son. She screamed hysterically as she saw my brother's eyes were open. The Indian's face was away from us and once again the wagon was lurching forward. The next thing I remember is everything being on top of us — all the things they had brought from their home so far away — all the belongings they had were now tipped upside down, because the wagon had rolled on its side. Mother managed to hold on to me, albeit with just one arm, but she was bleeding from her head. We were surrounded in upheaval, our clothes and little bits of furniture all about us in disarray. She must have been struck by something. Blood was trickling down quite badly from her forehead but her main concern was me. She could hear so much noise outside, horses whinnying, guns firing, her people crying and screaming. She stopped for a split second as if gathering her thoughts then decided to crawl out of the wagon, dragging me with her. I remained quiet. Mother crawled away towards the back of the wagon with one arm hanging on to me whilst the other arm was used to push away the things that had fallen everywhere. Tears were falling down her face and now panic had set in. She was trying to find Father. At the same time she had to hide me. Little did she know that whilst she was looking and searching for Father she was being watched. I saw her turn her face here and there, looking for somewhere safe to leave me. She opened the flap at the back of the wagon but turned away in fear. I knew she had seen something, something that made her feel all was lost once again. She crawled back out to me and went towards the front of the wagon, dragging me with her by my arm. I was crying now because her pulling was hurting me. Suddenly the smoke was becoming worse and after a few seconds Mother looked back to see it was coming from the back of our wagon, which was on fire.

The smoke was really strong and thick by now and as the wagon was on its side it was difficult for Mother to find a way out. Her fear was of other Indians out there, but she knew if we stayed in the wagon we would both be burnt to death, so she grabbed me in her arms tightly and pushed herself out, praying no one would see her. She rolled over and fell very close to the wagon. She was bleeding even more now as she lay with me next to the wheel of the wagon. She could hear horses but kept thinking of the wagon-wheel for she knew she could hide me by it if she covered me with things that had fallen out of the wagon. The fire at the back of the wagon must have been caused by an arrow, but because of the amount of smouldering dense smoke she knew the fire had gone out.

Her dress was long, down to her ankles. As she dragged herself towards the wheel she tore off her skirt to wrap around me. Then she put me amongst her now ruined belongings behind the wheel. The last things I remember about her were her fear but, above all, her love for me. She just looked at me, her hair very long, her face so dirty and as she came up close to me she kissed me and said, 'I love you, but I must look for your father. I know you do not understand at your tender age why I am leaving you, but I must.' She said all this as we were hidden behind the wheel. Of course, I did not understand, but I knew my mother expected to come back to me.

After Mother had hidden me as much as she could in such a short time she looked towards the wheel and the open space. Her skirt was now missing, just her petticoat was visible, but this didn't matter to her. Suddenly she spotted a small gun; where it came from she didn't know and she didn't really care, but she knew it could save her life. It was some yards away. Would she make it? She looked back to see I was right behind her and she laid her hand on me. Somehow I knew she would take the gamble and as she crawled away from me I watched her very closely. It was so clear, like everything else in the past few days had been. Where her strength came from I do not know, except maybe from fear. She crawled away from me but suddenly she stopped as if she had died. A horse with an Indian went by. I knew she was acting in the hope of fooling the Indian into believing she was dead. She edged forward a little, but within seconds an Indian was jumping down from his horse on top of Mother. He was pulling her hair and she was fighting and screaming, but there was no hope. He had a weapon in one hand and as he pulled her hair back her face was looking upwards. The scream was shattering and it was the last time I saw my mother's face. The Indian was walking away – in his hand was long, dark hair and there was blood on his hands.

The vision went – the smoke came back. I was once again with the Indian.

Apache Village

The village was big and by now I was seven years old. We were camped by a river where there were lots of trees. The other side of the camp was much more open land where the huts, as we called them, were built from leaves and branches. We played near the river and now and again played about in the water and thoroughly enjoyed ourselves. The weather was very hot and we knew that was the best way of keeping ourselves cool.

Suddenly I hurt my knee, I am not sure how it came about, but I do remember running back home, crying to my mother. My mother was sitting there, laughing at me, but at the same time had her arms outstretched to comfort me. She was a big woman and the dress she wore was folded up to the top of her legs, flapping between them. By now the other children had come out of the water to see if I was all right. Mother calmed me down and soon I was back playing with the other children. I had a younger sister and an older brother, and the three of us were playing ball happily and peacefully with all the other children in the village. There were only old men and women and children – I could see no young men – including my Father.

It seemed that all the young men had gone hunting, which left the old men to look after the women and children. My grandfather was near Mother as our huts were built close together. Some of the children were sitting at his feet as he told them wonderful stories of his adventures.

I looked at Mother and she called out, asking whether my knee was better. I waved and carried on playing happily.

All of a sudden I felt as if there was something wrong, I wasn't sure what, but I could sense it and from where I was playing I turned to look at Mother in the place where I had last seen her sitting down. She was now standing, shouting at us to come and, as there was such an urgent note in her voice, we knew we had to obey immediately. All the other children had also been called in and there was such an air of urgency and fear that some of the children began to cry, purely because of the desperation in their mothers' voices. The next thing I remember was that everybody was running about in all directions. I ran straight to my mother's arms, not knowing what was going on, she was still crying out to my brother and sister to hurry, and could see them coming. Beyond them I could see dust, lots of dust. Dust filled the air as many horsemen were riding towards us. I had seen this sort of thing when the men of our village rode out on hunting trips, but in my heart I knew that it was not my people this time coming home. These were White Men and there were many of them. I had never met a White Man before, though I was White as a baby, now I was Apache through and through – I felt Apache, I acted Apache – I knew danger was coming. My brother and sister had not reached my mother as quickly as I had and in her fear Mother cried, 'Run!'

The horsemen were coming in from the open land so I ran into the area of trees the river, for I knew there were big rocks there, ideal for hiding. Without hesitation, off I ran with all my might and as I ran I kept looking back to find that women and children were still running. The old men, and that included my own grandfather, were to stay to fight the White Man. How can an old man possibly win against a young man, be he White or Indian? These men had guns, our old men relied on their bows and arrows for protection. Before I reached cover amongst the trees and rocks I saw one of the old men of the village fall. I hear a lots of gun-fire. As I hid, I saw the White Men so clearly coming into the village. The terror they brought with them and the hate they had for the Indians, my people, showed in their eyes. White Men were jumping from their horses to run after our women while others were tearing the huts down. The men were dragging some women off to rape them and some women escaped, but then were very soon caught and raped on the spot while other Indians were being killed.

Suddenly, there were two children – not my brother or sister – but children of the camp, running through the trees. I shouted at them for I realised I was not in a safe place but knew where there was a suitable place to hide. I knew I had to follow the river and where I had to go, but before I could show them they shouted back at me, 'Look out! There are two White Men riding towards us!' There was a large rock with a huge split in it so we headed for cover. I managed to get to the rock first. I pushed myself hard in between the crack in the rock and my friends came beside me. All was silent. All we could hear after a couple of minutes were branches breaking, but we knew the White Men could not bring their horses into the trees. All we could do was to wait where we were, without making a sound, as we could hear them walking through the trees. My body was almost completely through the slit in the rock and I was trying to help one of my friends to come with me but the slit was not big enough. I could feel our bodies shaking and trembling but no sound was made. We had been taught to guard our lives – that was the White Spirit's way.

I was trying my best to follow the White Spirit's way, but in my heart I was petrified. Now there were more sounds, more branches broken and they were coming nearer. I was very well hidden from the outside but I could see through the slit of the rock. My young friends were trying to do the same, but to no avail for, suddenly, there was the White Man standing there. He grabbed my second friend with one hand and with the other he pointed a gun to his stomach and shot him. The other White Man pulled the girl out of the rock, and as he did so he and the other White Man were laughing, pushing the girl in between them. One of the men walked off, dragging the terrified girl behind him while his friend just stood there, shouting something which I couldn't understand. He did not see me so I made certain I kept as quiet as possible. In a short period of time I heard screaming. The man still stood there near to where I was hiding and then there was no sound at all. The other White Man appeared and as he stood next to his friend he wiped a knife on his trousers. The first man spoke, victoriously and proudly, 'That's finished. Let's go!' This time I could understand his words perfectly and I heard them leave. For a long time I waited there, not daring to leave the rock. Noises were still coming from the village, but were getting less and less now. Night was falling. I could not look at my poor friend any longer and knew I had to leave the rock and follow the river. I waited till there was no sound at all. It seemed for ever, and I waited till dawn until I was absolutely sure there was no one around who might be able to harm me. Even as I came out of the rock I had to see and look back as I walked.

My feet felt wet and as I looked down for a moment I thought I was seeing red sand. It was in fact red blood which came from where my dear friend had lain and died. I followed the trees back to our camp and, being taught the Apache way, I knew no one could see me. Had I walked out of the trees a White Man's way all that would have been in front of me would have been death, White Man's death. Every man, woman and child lay dead as I walked through, and as I searched for my mother a sense of hatred and loss was with me. Here I was, a child of seven who had been adopted and brought up by the Indians, taught to be brave and grown up before her time and yet, in the middle of all this, how could I be?

Eventually I managed to find Mother. She was in the hut and my grandfather was outside, face-down. I could tell it was Grandfather by his clothing and I was too frightened to go in at first but once again my upbringing came to the forefront. I had no fear at this stage and scoured the camp, looking at many women, many of whom were in such positions as to show they had been brutally raped. When I entered the hut I saw my sister lying spread-eagled on the floor, completely naked. Mother was sitting in the corner with her head bent down. I rushed to her, but as I touched her she fell forward. She was dead, too, as they all were.

I walked away and once again the Indian part of me came flooding back. I had to leave the ones I loved in case the White Man came back. I had no tears for I could show no emotion, I felt nothing. I was numb, for I had been so happy and now it had all gone. I walked back to the trees and the river which I knew so well.

The Sioux Village

Daylight was coming so I had to move quickly. Where to, I did not know, but I chose to follow the river. It was many days and nights of running and sleeping. I had been taught how to survive in the wilderness and I lived on fruits and berries of the wild. The river gave me water, the land gave me food so I knew I was safe from the White Man, for he did not know how to survive in the wilds. However, I knew that there where other dangers I had to watch out for. Although we were taught about the White Man, we were also taught about hostile Indians, Indians who were not of our tribe.

The knee I had injured at the river before the invasion was now hurting and began to swell as I walked and I realised that soon it would give up on me. That night I found some herbs from the ground and once again found a rock to hide and shelter me. I put the herbs on my knee and I knew I was running a fever due to the heat of my body. Whether it was because of my knee or something else — I did not care — I felt I had to lie down, hoping all would be well the following morning. I felt sure the herbs I had found would help. Sleep came upon me quickly.

Upon waking I found everything was quiet, and because I had suffered a fever all night and my knee was still painful, I was not as alert as I was brought up to be. As I walked out into the opening in the rock an Indian grabbed me. This was a different kind of Indian from any other I had seen. High up in the rocks were more of them on horses. My immediate concern was the Indian who stood next to me, so I bit him and tried to run off, but he grabbed me again. After what I had been through I was in no mood to give in easily again so I bit him again. However, this time he retaliated by hitting me with his hand, which made me see stars. As a rule, the Indian does not hit children, but this one had no choice. As I fell to the ground I looked up at him to see that he was looking up at the Indians who remained in the high rocks. I followed his eyes and it appeared that he focused them on one Indian, the Chief. The Chief lifted his arm high above his head, which was a signal that the Indian was to bring me and follow them all. My life had been spared — they had accepted me.

The Indian picked me up and put me on his horse. We followed the path up to where the group of Indians were waiting and as we reached them I looked at the Chief with such fear within me. He looked so powerful and his eyes just stared at me as he sat on his horse. One could tell he was about six feet tall, lithe and strong and yet graceful, very well-proportioned and with skin singularly clear and delicate. He wore no paint, his head was bare and his long hair was gathered in a clump at the back of his neck. His chest and arms were naked and a buffalo robe was hanging from his waist with a belt holding it in place. He was wearing different coloured moccasins on his feet. His eyes were proud and forceful, he did not smile – except now with his eyes. It was sign that all was well. They moved on and we seemed to be travelling for days. I cannot say for sure how many, but we would rest at night and then travel again by day. I knew the Sioux were not on their own land for some reason, and that they had been far away, so now they were going home. At night I would sleep on my own, but not far from their watchful eyes. Despite the fact they had accepted me, they still did not trust me.

The Chief would sit at night some yards from the other Indians, praying. Sometimes he talked to himself, which is something I had also noticed about the Apache men, and so I knew he was talking to White Spirit. The other Indians had great respect for this Indian and I knew he must be a big Chief. One night there was great talk of what to call me. I had to have a name, it seemed, but not the Apache name. After some discussion, one of the Indians came across to me to tell me that it was decided upon that my Sioux name was to be Little One. That night I also found out that the big Chief was called Sitting Bull, leader of the Sioux.

Soon I recognised excitement amongst them, and I knew their home was not far off. We were coming into new country now, different from what I had seen before. The land was vast with mountains, not as many trees as before, just open space. Suddenly, in front of me in the distance, I could see a village. It looked to me to be a big village with hundreds of huts. I was soon to find out that they were called teepees and they were different from what I had seen before. Looking away from the village I could see buffalo, many of them, and near the village was a river.

As we rode into the village there was much excitement, especially seeing the Chief. We rode through the village and I found many of its inhabitants looking at me, pointing and talking about me. The Chief continued and then stopped suddenly, then turned to speak to the Indian who was holding me. He pointed to a teepee and the Indian and I followed the Chief whilst the other Indians went their own way.

We dismounted the horse outside the teepee and I was told to follow the Chief, who went in first. I followed closely behind him and I could see an old squaw sitting there. The Chief spoke to her and, judging by their actions and gestures, it was concerning me. The old squaw had great respect for this man but I could tell straight away that she was not at all pleased with what he was saying. All of a sudden he turned without even looking at me, and left.

The teepee was large and very different from our huts, with paintings on the walls, rugs on the floor and the blankets were neatly rolled up around the inside of the teepee. The old squaw sat there, muttering to herself disdainfully for a good few minutes. I just stood there quietly, for I realised I was in a new land with new people. Even before she rose from her seated position on the rug I could see the hate in her eyes for me. I was a stranger from another kind of Indian tribe, but what made it worse was the fact that I was White. Having been brought up by the Apaches from a baby, I knew of no other life, but this made absolutely no difference to her. Yet I knew she would never harm me because the Chief had put me in her charge.

My hair was long and dark and as the squaw touched it she turned to pick something up, turned back and proceeded to cut it! There was no mention of telling me to sit down or anything and, as I watched the hair fall, my mind went back to my Apache brother whose hair was shorter than mine. I thought to myself, 'Now I will look like an Apache boy.' She left the teepee with me still standing there. I could hear lots of noises outside and voices but could not understand what was going on. The old squaw came back in and grabbed me and led me outside the teepee. It was still hot as we had ridden in early that afternoon and, what with the anxiety and the heat, sweat was making my clothes wet-through. The Indian with whom I had shared a horse was now sitting on the floor outside the teepee. I felt perhaps he had been put there to guard me but was not sure why. The squaw started walking towards the river which was near by, dragging me behind her. She was still muttering to herself, and she carried a blanket on the other arm. As soon as we got to the water's edge she walked in, dragging me with her. She threw the blanket back on to the riverbank and with both hands pushed me under the water! Not knowing if I was with friendly Indians or not, my first thought was that I was about to be killed by drowning, but within seconds she let go and I simply stood there, the water waist-high. She stood there tearing the little clothing I had been wearing into shreds and proceeded to wash me, first my hair, then my body. It seemed to go on and on for ever. Still without a word she turned away, dragging me with her towards the bank. She threw the blanket at me in almost a fit of temper and, before I had a chance to put it around me, off she went once again, with me in tow. When we arrived back at the teepee she put me inside, didn't utter one word to me and just left. I sat down, putting the blanket tightly around me. I was still trembling a bit with fear but felt much better after the river bath. I touched my hair which still felt strange.

From that day on I was to stay with this old squaw and I accepted that, too. The years with her were not so bad and the old squaw gradually learned to accept me, not like a true Sioux, but the colour of my skin now made little difference to her and day by day, year by year, her love for me was growing.

I did not see the Chief very often after that, and he certainly never came to visit me, but I respected him and loved him. I also knew he now accepted me as a Sioux girl and I was no longer a stranger.

Our camp moved many times over the years, sometimes coming back to places where we had been before. Many seasons came and went. I was growing up now and my hair had grown back to the normal long and dark familiar style. I grew to accept the old squaw as a mother figure and she taught me everything a young girl should know. I was coming up to the age of fifteen and growing up fast. I was fairly tall and slim and I wore my dress down to my ankles. I had many beads around my neck. I was beginning to show off to the young men of the village, but the *old squaw was quick to notice this and would tell me off. I did not understand this as there were other girls of the tribe marrying their men at my age, but she would only smile and say, 'There's plenty of time.'*

There was one man who seemed different from the rest. It was his eyes. I had seen eyes like his before and I remembered the Chief's eyes were the same as this young man's. I put two and two together and realised he was the Chief's son. I had not seen him many times because, like all the other young men of the village, he would go away for days on end hunting.

I would talk to the old squaw about him for in my heart I knew I liked him very much. The old squaw would say nothing but would always listen and smile.

As that year went by the boy was more and more on my mind. I would wait eagerly till the young men got back from their hunting trips, but then when I did manage to see him I would run away and hide, hoping he would not see my flushed face. Each time I saw him I felt excitement, and I gradually began to fall in love with him. He was so like his father, a strong, fine man.

Many evenings I would talk to the old squaw about him, but again she would say nothing except, 'Have patience, Little One.' However, one night she told me there was to be a wedding.

'Whose?' I asked.

'Yours, Little One. You are no longer a child, but a fine young woman. You will have to leave the teepee to join your husband.'

I was upset a little to learn this, as by now I loved the old squaw lady dearly. I asked her whom it was I was to marry, but all she said was, 'You will be told soon.' In my mind I went through all the young men of the village. I did not sleep very well that night, knowing I would not be happy. However, as it was the Indian way, I knew I had to accept whoever he was.

The following day there was a lot of activity in the camp. The old squaw had kept me inside the teepee all day and had rolled up all my belongings in a blanket. I was wearing a long, red dress and wore my hair swept back, which was black and shiny. I had more beads on this day than I had usually worn. I remembered the wedding dress that belonged to a young woman many moons ago. She had been scalped. It was the one and only time I remembered and, as quickly as the vision came, it went. I realised I was now an Indian woman.

We were once again camped near a river. There were teepees on both sides. It was a small river one could easily walk across. It was now late afternoon and the old squaw was fussing around me like a mother hen. I could sense the pride and excitement in her, but also knew she was sad for she had looked after me for so long. Suddenly I could hear horses outside the teepee and the old squaw stopped arranging my dress and left the teepee. I felt sick with a mixture of emotions – excitement, fear but also sadness – for I was to soon leave my home and the old squaw to start a new life with my husband, who was still unknown to me.

The flap of the teepee was then flung open and in walked the Chief. No one had told me that he would be involved with my wedding. All I had been told was that I was to marry that afternoon, and would simply have to move into my husband's teepee with his family, taking all my belongings with me. That was the marriage I had accepted, along with the usual feasting and exchanging of presents after the ceremony.

The Chief beckoned me to follow him outside, where there was an Indian on a horse waiting for me. He was holding another two horses' reins and the Chief helped me to climb up on to one of the horses. He got on his horse and took the lead, with the other Indian and I following him. I looked back over my shoulder at the old squaw, her face full of smiles because she knew it would not be very long before I was to find out which of the young men I was to wed.

We approached the river, passing many teepees on the way, and across the river I would see there were a few more of them scattered around, one of which belonged to the Chief. When we reached the river we all dismounted and the Chief pointed to one of the teepees across the river, telling me to go to it. With my belongings in my arms, I waded across the river and walked towards the teepee. Once more the sickness in my stomach came back as I did not know who was waiting there for me.

I was almost there when, suddenly, the flap of the teepee swung open and in front of me stood the Chief's son. He explained to me I had been promised to him by his father and that he wished me to be his wife. I understood now why the Chief himself had come to fetch me. The Chief's son held out his hand and, as I stood there looking at him, my mind flashed back to the many evenings I had spent with the old squaw speaking to her of him and how over the past twelve months I had fallen in love with him. There had never been any sign of his feelings, but here I was, now standing next to him, about to become his wife. His hair was long and tied back with a white feather hanging down at the back. He was wearing white buckskin trousers with a waistcoat to match and he had beads around his neck and armbands on his arms. His complexion was clear and he had no paint on his face or a body like most Sioux men. At the age of seventeen, he was very much a man, handsome with crystal blue eyes that looked at me as if he could see through me. He took my hand and I followed him into the teepee where we were to start our life together as man and wife. I was deliriously happy and realised now that the old squaw had known all along that this was the man I had been promised to, the man I loved so much.

Our life together was wonderful and I saw the Chief many times now that I was married to his son. My husband's name was White Feather and he was so like his father in lots of ways and very close to him. White Feather seemed to be his favourite son though, and we lived for a while with his family. After a short while we moved into our very own teepee. In the first year of our marriage I became pregnant. White Feather was very happy about the prospect of becoming a father. He was a very kind and gentle man but sometimes he had to go away, often for days and sometimes weeks at a time, to go on hunting trips. The child was due in the autumn and, as the days grew nearer, White Feather would stay closer to me, not going on his trips. I knew he really wanted a son although not once had he mentioned this to me. I was hoping it would be a boy for his sake. The baby was now due and White Feather, like any other father awaiting the safe arrival of his first child, was watching me all the time. The baby started coming in the middle of the night and White Feather called his mother for assistance. There was much going on around me but White Feather would not leave my side. Early in the morning our child was born, a beautiful little girl.

She was passed to White Feather and as I looked up to him I saw his eyes were full of pride as he held his first child. It did not matter to him that she was a girl and he was fully contented and fulfilled.

The following two years I was to have two more daughters and by now White Feather was becoming a Medicine Man. His father had been a great Medicine Man in his time and like all other Medicine Men he also had great vision of seeing spirit and predicting forthcoming events. The Sioux tribe was very spiritual and its people fully understood the power of spirit.

I was beginning to worry that I had not been able to bear a son for White Feather. He had been present at the births of each of his three daughters and now eagerly awaited a fine boy. Although he loved his daughters I knew there was a sadness in his eyes. On many occasions White Feather went away to the mountains to pray to the Great White Spirit and see visions.

Very shortly after our third child, I was expecting another baby and White Feather had once again gone away to sit among the mountains, and when he returned this time there was a renewed brightness in his eyes. He put his arms around me and swung me in the air. The White Spirit had spoken to White Feather to tell him that this time I was carrying a son. He was so happy that day as he played with his daughters, in the knowledge that a son would now be following in his footsteps as he had followed his father's. I sat on the river bed holding my youngest child in my arms while White Feather played with the children in the water. I watched him with such love and so glad to see him happy and pleased the White Spirit had given him so much joy. I was grateful to be able to share my life with such a good man and father to my children. He looked back at me and smiled with so much love that it was indeed a day to remember.

Days before I gave birth to my fourth child, White Feather was injured and needed constant nursing and attention. This went on for several days even after our baby was born. He was now too ill to know he had a son at last. He had been injured by an arrow during a bloody battle with a rival tribe from another village. An arrow had embedded itself in his body. Despite the agonising pain it caused him, White Feather carried on fighting, eventually killing the Chief of the other tribe, which was a great feat amongst the Indians. White Feather's father managed to get the arrowhead out of his son's body and made up a mixture of special healing herbs which he changed daily. Although he was very worried about White Feather, the Chief spoke to me of the immense bravery his son had shown. I was so proud but extremely worried about White Feather. Thankfully, he began to improve and get better again and slowly was able to sit up. I showed his newly born son to him and he was so proud. He thanked the White Spirit for this baby and, looking at me, he said, 'From now on I will be known as White Arrow in honour of my victory.' Gazing down on his little son he said, 'He will have my name, but instead of being known as White Feather he shall be called Small Feather.'

With White Arrow better, life carried on as normal. One evening we had an argument over something or other. He was preparing to go on another war party. Maybe I was worried about it. The following morning we were still not very happy with each other, and I had made up my mind not to help him with his preparations. I usually helped White Arrow with his warpaint, but this particular morning I decided to teach him a lesson and ignored him. When he went I felt sorry about our disagreement and thought to myself, When he comes back, I'll make it up to him.

Days later there was movement in the camp. Whereas it was normally so noisy with children playing and the people going about their everyday chores, suddenly it was deathly quiet. I could see the horses coming, the Chief at the head of them. In his hand he was holding a strap of another horse and, as he led this other horse into our village, I saw an Indian lying draped over it. I knew it was White Arrow and as the Chief brought him closer to me the vision faded away, very slowly till I could see no more.

Chapter 15

Now I am back in the present day and I am sitting in my living room, blinking my eyes and realising I am Ann Walker. It dawned on me why I had been so confused with the names of White Arrow and White Feather, and why there was such a closeness between White Arrow and myself, for we had been man and wife in a previous life.

As I looked across at Tony, who was still asleep, it was an odd situation to find myself in. Now I had two husbands to contend with.

During this period Tony's father was a regular visitor to us, and often appeared whilst we were in the car. I liked him very much and would often pass on messages to Tony from him. He appeared to like me, too, and we got on quite well. I saw Tony's mother once, but that was all. She came in one day and said only a few words before vanishing again. On one particular day we were driving to our favourite beauty spot called Little Britain, and Tony's father was sitting in the back of the car.

Suddenly, he said to me, 'This is where I caught the barbel,' and he pointed to the exact spot.

'Really?' I replied.

I told Tony his father was with us. 'Your Dad says it was over there where he caught that barbel fish,' and I pointed to the part of the river where he had shown me. We were parked alongside the river but behind us was also a large lake. I took it that his father meant he had caught the fish just where we were, when suddenly I saw beside our car a measuring pole sticking up out of the water.

Tony's father then said, 'There's a pole just like that one where I caught the fish,' and I repeated this information to Tony.

'No, you're wrong,' said Tony. 'It wasn't here, love, you are mistaken.'

I looked back at his Dad who was still sitting on the back seat.

'OK,' said his father, 'ask him if we caught the fish here or not.'

I asked Tony who replied, 'Yes, in these parts, but not where we are now.'

God, I thought. I wish I hadn't bothered telling him now, but I wasn't going to be beaten by something so stupid as this!

I asked Tony to show me exactly where his Dad had caught the fish.

'All right,' he said, and got out of the car. I got out, too and started to follow. I looked back at the car and said, 'I hope you're right,' and looked to see if his father was still there. I still hadn't got used to the spirit world completely, forgetting they don't need doors to get in and out of cars etc. when all of a sudden his Dad said, 'Don't worry, Ann. I am right,' and to my astonishment, he was walking right beside me! I still wasn't always prepared for when spirit turn up like that and I stopped in my tracks.

'What's the matter?' asked Tony.

'Nothing,' I replied. 'It's just that your Dad is here right next to me,' and I carried on following Tony.

After a short distance, Tony stopped and turned to look at me.

'It's just round the corner,' he said, and walked on.

For a moment I thought I'd let him carry on, I just knelt down by the river, looking at the swans. It was such a lovely day and it felt good to get away from work for a while. I began to throw stones into the water when I heard Tony call out, 'Ann!' His voice had a ring of excitement about it.

'Come here, quickly,' he said. 'I've got something to show you.'

I walked round the corner. It was fairly shady, but I could see the water clearly. Beside me stood the measuring pole which my father-in-law had told me about. Tony was aghast!

'All the times my father and I used to go fishing here there has never, ever been a measuring pole to my knowledge. Certainly never in this part of the river, anyway, for I know this section like the back of my hand and I swear I have never set eyes on that before!' Tony exclaimed.

He looked flabbergasted and wondered how on earth I knew all about the pole. I shrugged my shoulders and said, 'Well, your father did say where he had caught the fish and that there was a measuring pole.'

I didn't want to sound cocky, but I was really pleased that I had managed to prove his Dad right, or I should say his Dad proved himself right. At the same time I was surprised that Tony was still being a bit sceptical. But it was still early days for Tony, and after all, he couldn't see what I could see, nor hear what I could hear.

In the months that followed, there were many incidents like this which occurred, and Tony became absolutely convinced. White Arrow never left my side at any time. Whenever anyone else in spirit came into contact with me White Arrow would step back to let them closer, but would never leave me completely. I was at all times fully aware of his presence and Tony would ask White Arrow many questions through me.

One day, Tony was asking White Arrow something, when suddenly White Arrow replied, 'Ask my wife!'

Now, let me take this opportunity to explain. I don't give myself time to think whenever White Arrow speaks, I just repeat what he says and think about it afterwards. I could have bitten my tongue in this instance, for as soon as I said it Tony went very quiet and then asked me what White Arrow meant. My mind went back to the reincarnation and I knew White Arrow had really upset the apple cart. Now seemed the appropriate time to tell Tony about my reincarnation, so I explained the whole story to him. Let me tell you about Tony. He has always been a very possessive sort of man and, judging by the look on his face, I could tell that it didn't matter that White Arrow was a spirit or not, the very idea that some other man should call me his wife was not right. Tony had accepted White Arrow to a certain degree, but after that crack from White Arrow I wondered how long the friendship would last between the two men. I turned to White Arrow to have a go at him, but he had vanished.

'Come on, love,' I said to Tony. 'That happened well over a hundred years ago and my feelings for you are different from what I feel for him.'

I paused for a moment for I realised how daft this all was. Here we were, arguing over someone who was dead!

'Yes, maybe I'm being stupid,' said Tony, 'But you have to admit that he is calling you *his* wife, when you are *mine*.'

'Let's forget it, Tony, for goodness sake,' I said. 'It's not as if White Arrow is living and can run off with me!'

'By the way, where is White Arrow now?' he said.

'I don't know,' I said, but in my mind I thought, 'just you wait till I catch up with you!'

That night he didn't appear until very late. Tony was reading, and when I told him White Arrow was back he said, 'Don't you think you'd better have a word with him?'

I beckoned my finger at White Arrow and said, 'I want you. Where have you been all day? I've been waiting for you. I must have a word with you about what you said this afternoon.'

'Why?' asked White Arrow, grinning from ear to ear and acting the innocent.

'I don't think it's at all funny,' I said, keeping a straight face. 'You know perfectly well why. It's about you calling me your wife.'

White Arrow sat down on the floor and said, 'I know, but you are my wife. It's a habit I have of saying.'

'Well, I've never heard you say it before,' I said, 'but in any case could you please try not to say it again because it causes too much friction between Tony and me.'

White Arrow said he was just being awkward.

'Come on, White Arrow,' I said. 'You've got to try and understand Tony and his feelings, for it's all very strange to him. Although *I* understand, it will take Tony time, and remember I've got to live with the pair of you. Do you understand what I am saying? Poor Tony can't see who I am talking to or hear what they are saying to me, and it must be so difficult for him, without you piping in with comments like that one.'

He nodded and he wasn't being awkward now.

He said, 'I'm sorry, I promise I'll try not to say it again,' but as he got up to go his parting words were, 'but, you are my wife!!'

Life was getting good now and I was gradually becoming a different person. Everything around me looked different. I was noticing the flowers and trees, the animals and birds now, I had left work, too, which meant I now had more time for the spirit world. Mum was much happier too, as she could see a vast improvement in me, and she and the girls had accepted White Arrow completely. Likewise, White Arrow liked them and enjoyed the times when we went round to visit them. I was still taking four pills a day, but at least I hadn't gone backwards. The family had not mentioned it, but I knew they were glad that I had come as far as I had without taking a retrograde step. Mum and Tony were pleased because in the past I had always suffered from severe depressions and was often crying. Now I was much happier, contented, and looked better than I had done for years.

Although White Arrow was around me all the time, apart from the other spirit people popping in to say 'Hello', I had animals come to see me, too. This proved to me that our pets live on in the next world, which is a comforting thought.

One night I went to bed early. There was to be a film on television that I particularly wanted to watch. There had been a good write-up about it in the papers so I left Tony downstairs doing his paperwork and went upstairs to bed to watch television in comfort. As I got into bed and made myself comfy, the film started. I had left the bedroom door open, so if Tony shouted from downstairs I could hear him. As I leant back on my pillows and pulled the bedclothes around me the film started. Suddenly the sound of the voices in the film seemed to be fading away. I started to get up from my comfortable position to adjust the set when I noticed the smell of perfume in the room. The next thing I knew, I seemed to be drawn to the corner of the bedroom. A figure started to build up in front of me. It all happened in a matter of seconds and then, before me, stood a geisha girl. She was no more than nineteen years old and as she stood there I was taken aback by her looks. She was beautiful beyond words. She was about five foot three and had a slim figure. Her hair was thick and dark and it was piled high on her head and delicately adorned with ribbons, and what looked like ornamental sticks were holding it up in place. The coloured ribbons were attached to the sticks and were hanging down. The darkness of her hair showed up the colours of the ribbons beautifully and the sticks were red and yellow. In contrast, her face looked almost white, but I could see it was her make-up that made it appear so white. Her eyes were a deep shade of brown and her face was small with a gentle smile. Her dress looked very heavy and was made out of a deep mauve fabric with a flowery print all over it. It draped loosely down to her feet and she held her hands in front of her as if in prayer. Suddenly, she bowed to me and I could tell she was greeting me. She began to move closer to me and as she did so her perfume got stronger, the same perfume I had smelt in the room beforehand. I couldn't hear or see the television any more. Instead, my eyes watched every movement she made and I was totally entranced. I couldn't move as I watched her and after a couple of steps she stopped and stood still. I didn't know what she wanted and I didn't care, to be quite honest. I had seen geisha girls on the television before, but this was different. Here was one right in front of me and, to me, a very real person.

'Hello,' she said so quietly, I could only just hear her.

'Hello.'

I leant back on my pillows, and noticed her long well-manicured nails.

Gosh, you are lovely, I thought to myself, forgetting again that spirit can read our thoughts.

'Thank you,' came back her reply. 'Do you mind if I tell you my story?'

Usually the spirit world never bothered to ask me permission!

I said, 'Of course I don't mind. Please go ahead.' As she told me about her life on earth she had tears in her eyes. She told me all about a great love she had for a young European boy her father strongly disapproved of it. He stopped her from seeing him. However, because her love for the boy was so great she disobeyed her father. Unfortunately, her father found out and, with a firm warning, told her never to be disobedient again.

The following week the European boy and the geisha girl ran away together, but it wasn't long before her father and some of the family caught up with them. This resulted in a terrible argument and fighting broke out, during which the young boy was killed by a knife wound. The poor girl was heartbroken and this explained why she had tears in her eyes as she spoke to me. She was then sent away to another part of the country to relations, but she couldn't forget the European boy whom she loved so dearly. She gradually became so depressed that she decided to take her own life so that she could join him in the next world.

At this point I stopped her to ask how she died, but she wouldn't tell me. I didn't wish to pursue the matter further, but I asked her if she did manage to join her loved one. She said she did. I was happy for her and told her so.

She said very quietly, 'Thank you for listening to me,' and with that she slowly faded away until I could see her no longer.

All this time the television was still on. The geisha girl had only been with me for a little while and when I looked back, with a view to following the story of the film, I found I had no interest in it, for my mind was still on the geisha girl, and I was glad. I had missed the film after all, for I was so delighted that I had had the privilege of meeting her. When I settled myself down to sleep later that night I hoped that I would meet her again some day.

One morning, Mum telephoned to say she had the day off and would I like to pop round. I glanced up at the clock to find it had just gone past ten, so I had plenty of time before Tony would be home for his lunch. That gave me a couple of hours to spend with Mum and I was looking forward to it. It was sunny outside so I decided to put on a jacket instead of a coat and slammed the front door behind me before I walked up the garden path.

All of a sudden, I saw my dog Sally down at my feet. I stopped in my tracks because for a second I could hardly believe my eyes. I looked again, just to make sure, and there she was. My mind went back to my early years and the times we had shared together. By this stage I had learned that it was only me who could see the spirit world and that I couldn't speak out loud to a spirit when I saw one, otherwise people in the living would think I was talking to myself. Therefore, quietly in my mind, I said, 'Hello, Sally,' and with that her tail started wagging. I felt so choked when she did that, for I would have dearly loved to cuddle her, but I knew it was impossible. As I walked out of the gate, I wondered if she would follow me or just simply disappear but, to my delight, she followed me all the way to Mum's house. Then as soon as I reached the door she disappeared. I felt sad for a moment, and hoped it wouldn't be the last time I would see her.

When it was time for me to leave Mum's house, I started to look for Sally straight away, but she wasn't there. On my way home I had to call in at the paper shop for a paper and some cigarettes. As I came out there was Sally sitting on the pavement, waiting for me. I had to check myself once again, as I had often done, for I still wasn't used to telling the difference between the living and the dead.

As I walked off she followed me, but when I arrived back home she vanished again. This carried on for a few weeks, but after that I didn't see her for some time, and she doesn't stay long nowadays, but I'm always glad to see her occasionally and truly grateful that she hasn't forgotten me.

Life in general was going along fine with White Arrow by my side and every day I learned something new. For the first time in my life I was on top of the world. One day I was with Mum. I loved her and am proud to admit it, for she was a good woman and I don't think a mother and a daughter could ever be closer than we are. We were enjoying life now in a way we never thought possible, and I was as well as could be expected. Both Mum and Tony were proud that I had come this far and that for months now I had stayed that way; they were both convinced I was almost cured of the drugs. Therefore, nobody bothered about the four pills a day I was taking, that is, until that afternoon. I made myself a cup of tea, switched on the television when suddenly White Arrow appeared.

White Arrow often appeared whenever I was sitting watching television. I gathered that this media had been an easy way for him to pick up the English language, and I was amused that he was able to learn in this manner. I never commented on it, but let him get on with it and I would carry on watching whatever programme was on with him. On this particular day to my surprise I heard White Arrow say, 'Turn it off.'

I looked at him questioningly, but leant forward to turn it off, nevertheless. 'What's the problem?' I asked as I lit a cigarette. I leant back on the armchair. It was so unlike White Arrow to order me about. 'Ann,' he said.

'Yes?'

'What about the pills?'

Not once had White Arrow ever brought up the subject of my drug-taking and I was taken aback. The only thing I could say was, 'Well, what about them?'

'Isn't it about time you stopped taking them, for they don't belong in the future.'

I sat still, feeling slightly stunned for a moment. I hadn't really considered that four pills a day would cause me any harm, but I knew he was right. The truth was, I didn't really want to let go of them. They had always protected me from being hurt. By now in return I had stopped hurting my family.

Once again White Arrow repeated that they didn't belong in the future.

'I know,' I replied. I thought to myself that to many people four pills a day would be nothing to cry about, but these were not normal pills and for twenty-three years I had been addicted to them. I honestly didn't want to stop taking them, the very thought terrified me. I wished White Arrow hadn't brought the subject up because since I had met him I had been so happy and contented and I didn't want anything to spoil that.

As I looked up at him I knew I should have expected him to want me to stop taking them and, although my family hadn't talked about it to me for ages, I knew deep down that soon they might very well ask the same thing. My mind went back to Dad, when it had all started, and just then I was terribly frightened.

I was forgetting White Arrow could read my mind. He said, 'Do you trust me, Little One?' He was speaking softly now.

'You know I do,' I replied, 'But what if . . .'

Before I could finish the sentence, White Arrow interrupted and said, 'If what, Ann? You can do it. Trust me.'

I knew he wouldn't let me down, but I just couldn't help being scared.

White Arrow said, 'Every day won't be like heaven and I won't lie to you, but many good things are in store for you and you will not need or desire the pills any more. The time has come for you to come off them, so you will be ready for these things that will happen to you in the future.'

My mind went back to when I had first turned to God for help, to that church visit. During the wonderful period in my life that I had White Arrow by my side I had never considered that God might have listened to my cry and given me the greatest gift of all. For the first time I said, 'Thank you,' and what White Arrow was asking of me seemed such a small request compared with what God had given me.

'OK,' I said. 'I can't promise, but I'll try my best.'

White Arrow smiled and I knew I had his strength to back me up. I wanted to prove to my family I could get well, but I had let them down so often. I prayed that this time I would succeed.

Since coming to Hillingdon to live, I had signed on with a doctor who had been quite willing to allow me to stay on that daily dosage, but White Arrow suggested that I should find a new doctor who would help me come off them completely, who would have the patience and conviction to help me come off them instead of giving me the easy option. I don't doubt that White Arrow had something to do with the fact that I was able to find the right doctor, for he turned out to be helpful and understanding. At the beginning he asked to see me every other day, and slowly but surely started cutting down the pills by just a quarter of a pill a week. During that time White Arrow was always there, and if I felt depressed he would cheer me up.

Very often when Tony came home from work in the evening he took me out and sometimes we went on to see friends after we had visited Mum and the kids. Sometimes we went for long drives, and I found that with the full support of both Tony and White Arrow, I was winning. The only problem I encountered at this stage was that I was not sleeping at all well and often I was still wide awake at four in the morning.

It was during these restless times when White Arrow would take me back to the past life I had spent with him in North America. After a while it always had the desired effect and I gradually drifted off to sleep.

As White Arrow is my guide from the spirit world, he has taught me that everyone on this earth has their own guide, like him.

Sometimes these guides are referred to as door-keepers and they are linked with you and stay with you from the time you are born till the day you die. There are also some spirit people who are known as helpers. Sometimes they stay with us a long time, sometimes just for a short period – it all depends on our needs at the time – but they are just as important in their own right as are our guides. As a rule, guides and helpers are not members of our spirit families but more highly evolved beings. One night, as I was getting ready for bed, a nun appeared. She wasn't very tall and was a little on the plump side. I would say she was about fifty or sixty years old, and the wonderful feeling of peace which I felt in her presence was remarkable. She said in a very quiet, soft voice, 'I've come to help you, my child.'

'Thank you.' I replied, not really understanding what kind of help she was referring to. However, I was very pleased to see her and I adored the serenity she brought with her. I asked her to tell me her name and she said it was Sister Maria.

She said, 'I've come to give help to you at night for your sleep.'

Before I could reply she said, 'Trust White Arrow. He has called on me for my assistance with this problem of yours.'

That made me feel much happier, for I was worried at first that she meant White Arrow was going away and it was the first time since the beginning that such a thought had entered my head, and I didn't like the prospect of not having him around one bit. What if he did go one day? What would I do? How would I feel and how could I go on without him? All these fears and questions went through my head. All of a sudden White Arrow appeared and sat on my bed. Sister Maria remained standing at the side of my bed just listening. Just then I became very overcome with emotion and tears began to come to my eyes. 'Don't ever leave me, will you White Arrow?'

'Little One, he replied, 'while you are on this earth I will be by your side every waking day. You have trusted me so far and I tell you now I am your guide for ever, so take the tears and fears away now. From now on and until you are sleeping properly again, Sister Maria will be with you one night and I the next. She is here to help you, so trust her as you do me.' Before he left he turned and said to me, Remember, Little One, I'm at your side, always.'

I was happy now he had said that and I turned to speak to Sister Maria.

'I'm so sorry,' I said. 'I didn't mean to sound disrespectful.'

'I understand completely, think nothing of it,' she replied.

When it was time for me to turn the light out I wondered how long I would lie there, waiting for sleep to come. Suddenly, Sister Maria took me out of my body and far away to a convent. I found myself with all the nuns and we were all praying together. After our prayers we all walked towards our bedrooms and as I walked into one of the rooms I thought to myself how bare they looked. All it had was a cross on the wall and a single bed, and by the side of the bed was a small table. On the table was a side light and a Bible. The sensation of peace and tranquillity in that little room was very strong and I got into bed, picked up the Bible and held it to my chest. I didn't read it but lay my head back on the pillow and before I knew it I drifted off to sleep.

The following morning, on waking, I remembered it all and thanked Sister Maria. Over the coming months White Arrow and Sister Maria managed to get me off to sleep normally and I no longer needed their little trips away to settle me.

During this period something happened which showed the other side of White Arrow. Let me explain – although most nights I was now sleeping better – there were the odd occasions when I wasn't, and this particular weekend, no matter what White Arrow or Sister Maria did to try to help me, it didn't seem to work. I was almost off the pills, but not quite, and on the Monday which followed this bad weekend I didn't feel at all well.

I said to Tony, 'We'll have an early night tonight as I haven't been sleeping too well the past two nights.'

Tony said, 'OK. You go up and I'll bring you up a hot drink in a minute.'

'Thanks, love,' I said and went upstairs. As I was walking up the stairs White Arrow appeared and said to me, 'Will you go and get some paper and a pen?'

I thought, What on earth should he want me to do that for? I wasn't really in the mood, but I thought, Anything for a peaceful night's sleep.

As I went back downstairs again, Tony said, 'What's the matter?'

'White Arrow wants me write something down.'

'What sort of thing?' asked Tony.

'I haven't the faintest idea. With White Arrow you never know what he wants, it could be anything.'

Tony laughed. 'You'd better go up and see. 'I'll be up in a while,' he shouted as I turned the corner at the top of the staircase.

As I climbed into my bed White Arrow was sitting on Tony's bed waiting for me. I said to him, 'OK, I've got the paper and pen. What's it all about?' I really hadn't a clue what he had in mind so I was quite intrigued.

Just then, a Cherokee Indian appeared and stood next to White Arrow. They exchanged words but I couldn't hear them. After a couple of minutes I got a bit impatient and said, 'Come on, White Arrow, I'm tired,' but he completely ignored me and carried on talking to the Cherokee. This continued for about five minutes and then White Arrow looked at me and started to tell me what to do. He told me to draw a picture which he would describe in detail, which would be an Indian symbol. When I finished it I looked at White Arrow, waiting for him to carry on with further instructions, but he said, 'That's it!' and with that both he and the Cherokee vanished. About half an hour later White Arrow returned but was on his own this time. By now, Tony had come up to bed, and I was sitting up having the drink he had made for me.

'What was all that about?' I asked White Arrow.

His only answer was, 'It's important,' and with that he vanished again.

I had given up trying to solve this baffling guessing game and all I wanted to do was try to get some sleep. Although Sister Maria was with me I could not concentrate on going away to the convent with her, so I knew I was going to have another bad night. Sure enough, the following day I felt rough. I had gone for three consecutive nights with hardly any sleep and it had really got to me.

I said to Tony, 'If I don't sleep tonight I'll have to see the doctor for some advice.'

Tony was a bit surprised as he knew my sleeping had been bad, but he didn't like the thought of the doctor putting me back on more pills. I was, after all, almost off them completely now and it would be such a pity to have to go backwards.

'It's OK, Tony, I don't want more pills, I just need a bit of help. After all, I must sleep.'

Tony stopped worrying then. White Arrow was around most of that day then early in the evening he vanished again. I had an early night and had only been in bed ten minutes when back he came with the same Cherokee. I had had a suspicion that I would be in for a repeat performance somehow so I had already brought the paper and pen upstairs. This time White Arrow didn't have to talk with the Cherokee and I presume it was because they had spoken before they came to me. I had already told Tony about the previous night, so I turned to him as we sat up in bed and said to him, 'They're here again, Tony.' Tony said nothing, he only smiled and carried on watching television. White Arrow once again told me to draw a picture of an Indian symbol as he described it, as he had done the night before. Never before had White Arrow needed help with a message such as this. I went to sleep and put the symbols in the drawer for safe keeping. Again, I had a bad night, so the following morning I made an appointment to see the doctor. Tony took me by car and on the way there White Arrow sat in the back. This was nothing unusual for him, but he didn't seem very happy for some reason or another, going by the expression on his face. I didn't take much notice as I wasn't that happy myself, having lost so much sleep. What I did find strange, though, was that White Arrow followed me right into the doctor's surgery. Never before had he ever done such a thing and because he looked so annoyed as we sat waiting to see the doctor, I wondered if it was because he didn't like the idea of me consulting him, and possibly being prescribed some drugs to help me sleep.

'Look here, you've got to understand, White Arrow,' I said. 'I can't go on without sleep for this long. I know and appreciate your and Sister Maria's help. It has been invaluable and has worked up until a few nights ago, but I feel now I'm at the end of my tether and can't cope any longer. Please understand.'

He said nothing. I thought to myself, Please yourself!

At last it was my turn to see the doctor and as I entered the doctor's room White Arrow followed me. The doctor was very helpful and, taking my case history into consideration, he prescribed some sleeping pills which were not addictive. I left the surgery thinking, Well at least I'll get a few nights' rest and then it will sort itself out. As I got back in our car White Arrow was sitting on the back seat, mumbling away to himself in his native tongue. This was the first time I had ever heard him speak in his own language and I could tell he was very angry. As I could not understand what he was saying, however, I did not know why. I said to him, 'If you're going to persist in speaking to me in your own language and not mine, we're going to get nowhere, are we?' He shut up for a second and I went on, 'Well? Are we?'

White Arrow said, 'Doctors are a waste of time, the symbols are far more important.'

First of all I was enraged by his remark and said, 'Hold it, White Arrow! Surely my sleep comes first.'

'No!' he retorted. 'The symbols are more important,' and he carried on mumbling to himself once more. I had never seen him like this before and I didn't seem to be doing a very good job of snapping him out of it. Suddenly, from nowhere, an Indian Chief appeared and sat right next to White Arrow. My memories of my reincarnation all came flooding back and I instantly recognised White Arrow's father. I was so pleased to see him! He spoke to White Arrow in their native tongue and after a short while the Chief looked up at me and smiled. I hadn't forgotten those eyes which were so like his son's, then, as quickly as he appeared, he vanished.

White Arrow had calmed down quite a bit by now. He said, 'I'm sorry, Little One, but the symbols are so important for you and we only have a short time in which you have to receive them all.' From that statement I gathered the Cherokee was to leave soon, but also realised that there were more to come. How many more I wasn't sure.

Everything went back to normal for the rest of that day and I wondered if I would ever see White Arrow's father again. I asked White Arrow what his father had said to him when they were sitting next to each other in our car, and he just intimated that it wasn't very pleasant for him! So I knew he had been told off, but I wasn't satisfied with that answer and curious to know exactly what he had said.

'Come on, White Arrow, you can tell me.'

'Well, besides upsetting you, Little One, my Father told me I was forgetting that I was spirit and not of the living.'

I understood what he meant, White Arrow had seemed many times to forget he was spirit! Despite all this, however, I felt sorry for White Arrow and told him so. 'I prefer you just the way you are.'

'Thanks, Little One,' said White Arrow, 'but I have to take notice and obey him.'

By this time I had got to know White Arrow only too well, so I knew he would soon forget the ticking off he had received from his father and be his old self again so I was not unduly worried.

That night and the following two nights I received a symbol, so by Friday I had five altogether. Apart from knowing they were very important, I didn't know any of their meanings. I kept them safely away in a drawer and nothing more was heard or seen of the Cherokee.

In the days that followed I was becoming more curious about the meaning and significance of the symbols so I said to Tony, 'Do me a favour and take me to some libraries to pick up some books on Red Indians?'

'Why?'

'Well, I think I'll try to find out if any of the symbols are in any of the books and if they are they might give some explanation as to their meaning.'

Tony is fairly easy going and agreed. What we had not envisaged was how many Red Indian books there are available. It took me three whole months to read all I could about the Indians, but I didn't come across anything resembling the symbols I was looking for.

One day an idea came into my head and I suggested that Tony and I go to the British Museum. By this stage I think poor Tony had had enough of Indians to last him a lifetime so I reassured him by saying, 'I promise you that if I have no luck at the British Museum with what I'm trying to find, I'll give up.'

He laughed and said, 'I've heard that one before!' But when we got there we did manage to find a book on Indian symbols. The author's name was Jefferson and in the book we found very similar drawings to those which I had. In fact, they were almost identical. Unfortunately, that's where our luck ran out, for there was no explanation whatsoever with them. I cannot say I wasn't feeling disappointed.

On the way home I asked White Arrow, 'Why don't you tell me what they mean?'

'One day, Little One, you will know the meaning of the symbols, but not now.'

I must admit that none of the reading was a waste of time for I had learnt such a lot about the Red Indians. I still had some Indian books at home and decided to finish reading them before taking them back to the library. I spent most of the following Sunday stretched out on the floor reading. Then I heard Tony get up to go to the kitchen.

'Do you want anything, love?' I called out.

'No, it's all right,' he said.

I carried on reading and when Tony came back into the sitting room he sat on the settee. I looked up at him and was just about to say, 'Are you OK, love?' when I spotted White Arrow. There he was, standing over Tony with a perplexed look upon his face. In his hands Tony was holding a bowl, but what was in it I couldn't see. Then White Arrow bent down on his knees, peering into the bowl that Tony was eating from. I was so amused by this that I had to put the book down and sit up to see what White Arrow was up to. Tony asked, 'What's the matter?'

I said, 'White Arrow seems intrigued with whatever it is you're eating.'

'It's only a grapefruit,' he said.

I asked White Arrow what was wrong, to which he replied, 'It's all right, Tony's explained what it is he's eating. I've never seen one before.'

I thought to myself, Well there's no reason why White Arrow should have seen one before and this was a prime example of the many things which White Arrow would come across which puzzled him, but Tony and I would be able to explain things to him which he did not understand before. I carried on reading the book. I had just eight pages left to finish when I found I had to close it for some reason or another.

I was delighted that Tony, Mum and the kids were used to White Arrow now and there was never any question about him being there. It wouldn't be long before I would need no more pills at all. One day my doctor said to me, 'You'll be completely off them in a couple of weeks, Ann.' You can't imagine how good it was to hear those words. When I went back to see the doctor in September, sure enough, he said, 'No more of your pills, Ann, they have been taken off the market.'

I knew that White Arrow had known this would happen. I walked out of his surgery, wondering to myself if I would be able to cope. Suddenly, White Arrow was there by my side and said, 'Little One, you'll never look back, so go home and tell your family that for the first time there will be no more pills ever again. Between you and me, Little One, we will overcome whatever comes our way.'

I found it easy to convince myself everything would be all right but Mum, love her, I knew would wait for more time to pass before she was one hundred per cent sure. I knew I had a couple of years ahead of me to prove I would stay off the pills.

In the following months I still had regular check-ups and consultations with my doctor, but overall I was a happier person. The one person I had to prove myself to was my dear mother, for I owed her more than anyone else on this earth. Tony always knew this, even before I met White Arrow, and had always understood the bond between Mum and me. White Arrow also knew how close Mum and I were and he was as pleased as I was when I saw the trusting look on Mum's face each time I saw her.

She had so much faith in me and I wouldn't, *couldn't*, let her down. We all love our mums and they are all special in their own right, but, because of the hard times Mum and I had shared, we were especially close. For me to be able to leave all the drugs behind me was the best present I could possibly give her.

One night, when I'd gone round to see her and the kids, and we were all sitting in the kitchen – our favourite chatting place – I asked her, 'Mum, are you pleased with me?'

'Ann, I loved you as you were and I will always love you. The only difference now is that I'm proud of you, too. Even with White Arrow being with you I know how difficult it has been for you to get used to no drugs and how bad the pain has been for you to withstand, but I know you better than anyone else, including White Arrow. I always knew that one day something would come along for all us to benefit, something which would take you off the drugs, and for that reason I thank White Arrow from the bottom of my heart. I know how much strength you receive from him and I knew that one day you would prove to me that you would be able to live without them completely.'

I was very moved by her kind words and, as we put our arms around each other, I sobbed, 'Oh, I love you, Mum,' and she repeated the words, 'I'm proud of you, Ann.'

We sat down again and composed ourselves. 'What about the girls, Mum? Do you think they'll trust me?' Karen and I were still not as close as Joyce and I. Almost as if she was reading my mind, Mum said, 'Give her time, love.'

I said, 'I don't think I'll ever be able to make up those lost years to both of them. It doesn't seem possible that Karen is now nineteen and Joyce is sixteen, does it?'

Mum said, 'Do you love them more than anything in this world?'

I said, 'Of course I do.'

'Then you will fight to prove it to them in the years to come.'

I couldn't help thinking, Yes, but how many years will it take?

Mum leant forward to hold my hand: 'No matter what you were, Ann, you were a good daughter and you tried your best to be a mother. It isn't too late to prove it to them.'

Out of all my doubts and fears I still had White Arrow. He reminded me that he would always be there to overcome any obstacles that arose.

Chapter 16

One Sunday evening Tony and I decided to go to church.

White Arrow said to me, 'Little One, do you remember the night Sister Maria came and you were frightened I would leave you?'

'Yes,' I replied, 'I shall never forget it.'

'Well,' said White Arrow. 'Everyone who is put on this earth has, from God, what you have got. That is, a guide to protect and look after you, as I am your guide. We are always with you to overcome whatever is to come.'

A question entered my head, one I hadn't thought to ask before. I asked White Arrow where he had been all my life. Why now, after thirty-seven years of hell? Where had White Arrow been all those years and why had he not helped me then? Maybe if he had done so then I wouldn't have to prove myself to the kids now. Maybe Tony and Mum wouldn't have had to go through hell and back. I was getting myself in a right old state with maybe this and maybe that . . .

The service was coming to a close by now and people were starting to chatter amongst themselves. Some of them were talking to us, but I wasn't concentrating on what they were saying to me. It was no good, I would have to continue my questioning of White Arrow later. I was dying to get home and sit down with White Arrow to finish our conversation there. There were so many answers and explanations I needed from him.

When we got home I went straight to bed, telling Tony that I was going to have a few words with White Arrow. Tony asked if they were important questions I was going to put to him and I said firmly, 'Yes, very.' As I said it, I took a good look at my husband. Not once had I really asked him if all this had bothered him. Our world had turned round this way and that for the past year and a half and I thought it was about time I considered him more, so I sat down with Tony before I went upstairs to talk with White Arrow. True enough, Tony had always seemed happy with what was going on, never questioning me, nor asking me how I felt having White Arrow in my life. I had always involved Tony in everything that had been said to me by the spirit world, and White Arrow in particular, but now, for the first time, I was asking, Was it enough? Tony had been with me from the age of sixteen and now he was seeing a different me. I wondered if he was happy with the changed me? Did he like me like this?

'What's the matter?' said Tony. 'I thought you were going to bed.'

'I'm thinking,' I said.

'What about?' he asked.

'You, Tony, you.' I said. 'I'd like you to sit down with me for a moment. I'd like to talk to you about something.'

'Give me two minutes and I'll be with you,' said Tony, and he got up to go into the kitchen to make himself a cup of tea. After he had put the kettle on he said, 'What's on your mind? You've been quiet ever since we left church.'

'I've never really asked you how you feel about all of this, about my new life with the spirit world and especially White Arrow.'

'Well,' Tony replied, 'I must admit when you first met White Arrow I wasn't at all sure about it, but now you are so well these days, and knowing White Arrow as well as I do now, I really don't mind. After all, you are still mine – nothing at all will ever change that. White Arrow is regarded as one of the family and I like him. That's all there is to it, so don't worry.'

I gave Tony a kiss and got up to go upstairs. He touched my hand and said, 'You have no need to worry at all, Ann, I love them as much as you do. I'd soon tell you if I was unhappy and I'm not.

I was learning more about the spirit world. When we die, although we go to heaven, that doesn't mean that we come back to see our loved ones with wings on our backs! We are the same people as we were on earth. White Arrow proved to me he was just like that. He had his moods on earth and they were no different now he was living in heaven, I can assure you! By the time I got to bed, sure enough, White Arrow was in one of his bad moods. There he was, lying on Tony's bed with both arms and legs crossed. 'Finished now?' he asked sarcastically. Patience is not one of his best qualities.

'Come on, White Arrow, I'm not in the mood for this. If you like, I'll ask the questions tomorrow when you are in a better frame of mind.' But really I hoping he wouldn't go, and once again I was forgetting he could read my mind. He smiled and sat up.

'OK –,' he said, 'out with it.'

'Why didn't you show yourself all those years ago when I needed you most of all? Why after thirty-seven years and not before?'

'Little One, from the day you were born I have been with you. I only wish I could have shown myself to you on many occasions. I wanted to, but there is law and order up there,' he pointed upwards, 'and I was not allowed to make you aware of my presence until now. You must know by now that very soon you will have to help other people through me. You wouldn't be of any use to them if you had not experienced the pain and suffering they will have had.'

I said, 'OK, I agree that perhaps there was a reason for my suffering, but why my family? That's the bit that hurts me most of all.'

'I know,' replied White Arrow. 'But it is all part of the plan to test everyone who is put on this earth. They each have a pathway to follow. Did you know you choose your own life?'

I laughed at this and said, 'What?! You're joking. Only a fool would pick mine!'

'You did, you know,' said White Arrow.

What he said was a bit hard to swallow, so I sat there for a few moments thinking back over my life and wondered if he could be right in what he said. Would I have looked and seen that I was going to be a medium myself in the knowledge White Arrow was going to be there, right alongside me? What I did know to be true was that I was pleased I had Mum, Tony and the kids and wouldn't have changed that part of my life. I would have definitely chosen all of them.

'Yes, maybe you're right,' I said to White Arrow. I knew he was speaking the truth and it made me feel a little bit humble to think my family had also chosen me, even if they were unaware of it.

'Before you go, White Arrow, there's one more thing I'd like to know. Will I be able to make it up to the family for all those years of unhappiness?'

'Yes, Little One, but it will not always be easy. You will have to give more time for the children to forgive and forget.' I understood that and now I had renewed strength to wait – the strength of White Arrow.

I heard Tony coming up the stairs and as White Arrow got up from Tony's bed he said, 'See you tomorrow, Little One,' then he vanished.

When Tony came into the bedroom he said, 'Did you ask your questions and, more to the point, did you get the answers you wanted?'

I explained what I had asked, and why, and White Arrow's answers to them.

'It makes sense,' said Tony.

I said, 'But there are so many other things I have to find out about.'

'I'm sure in good time White Arrow will tell you all you need to know,' said Tony reassuringly, and with that we both got into bed and went to sleep.

At last I was completely cured of all drugs and was enjoying life to the full. White Arrow was now part of the family and life continued that way. White Arrow had been with me for two years now and I had enjoyed every minute of it. One Sunday, White Arrow came in and sat down. Suddenly, he said, 'Little One, the time is coming up for us to help other people.' As much as I loved White Arrow, I knew I could not keep him to myself and my immediate family. I knew his real purpose for being here was to help people through me. I had very mixed feelings, because I didn't really want to share him any more than I would like to share Tony, then again I felt a bit selfish, for, after all White Arrow had done so much for me – why shouldn't I let others share some of my happiness? It was only fair.

I apologised to White Arrow for my feelings of selfishness and he smiled and I admitted I would be terribly nervous seeing people. 'It's not that I don't trust you, you know I do, and I know you'll take care of everything, but I can't help being apprehensive about the whole idea,' I said.

'I understand, Little One, but so many people on this earth need our help from the spirit world and that is the main purpose of my being here. As much as I love you and your family, always remember I am here, but not only for you and your loved ones but also because I must help the people in your world.'

I said, 'You're forgetting one thing though, White Arrow. Only the family and close friends know I'm a medium and that I work with you.'

'Leave that to me, Little One,' White Arrow said, without concern.

Tony was sitting in the armchair so I turned to him and said, 'Do you know what White Arrow has just told me, Tony? He wants me to start seeing people, that is, strangers, people I haven't met before.'

Tony looked surprised: it wasn't that he didn't trust White Arrow's ability to tell the truth, but he hadn't really expected it to happen so quickly.

He said to me, 'Will you cope, do you think?'

'I don't know,' I replied. 'But I have to try for White Arrow's sake. He needs to see the people on this earth, he says that's his whole purpose of being here. I'm so nervous at the very thought of it.'

'Don't worry, Ann,' said Tony. 'White Arrow has always looked after you and he always seems to know what he's doing.'

Tony has always had the greatest respect for White Arrow and trusts him totally. It was a great feeling to think Tony had faith in me, too, and I loved him for that.

The following day when White Arrow appeared I was in the middle of deep concentration, questions buzzing around in my head, so I asked White Arrow how it was he intended getting people here to see me. Once again he sat down and said, 'I will explain, Little One. Everyone on earth has a family in the spirit world and they know when the people on earth have troubled times. They are able to help as much as they can without the knowledge of their loved ones on earth. If, at times, they feel their guidance isn't enough it is then that they direct the people on earth to a medium. This is also very often carried out without them realising that their spirit family is responsible for this procedure. It is at this point that you come in, for you will be used as an instrument for guides like myself so we can speak through you in order to help these people. There are many forms of help we can provide, but what is most important is the fact that we are able to assist them in the first place. There are primarily two main reasons why people will wish to come to see you: either they may have lost loved ones and are perhaps left with a feeling of great grief, and need to have proof of life eternal, or else they have a problem and need advice with it.

'When the sitter arrives and their loved ones from the spirit world come to join them through their love, they are assured that their deeply departed loved ones never leave them. Of course they have work to do on the other side, but if help is needed at any time they are there at once and do not need to be asked twice. It is most important that the people in your world know that their loved ones are still living, albeit in the next world, and will do all they can to help. When these spirit people were living on your earth their families and friends would go to them for help and yet, after they come to my world, it appears the need for their advice ends. It is such a shame when this happens, for why ignore a loved one because you cannot see them?

'So our prime reason for working this way is to prove the existence of my world and that we may give proof of survival. Whatever it is that people are searching for, myself and other guides are here in order to try our best to put them on the right path. It is irrelevant whether their problem be simple or major, whatever it is, they have come to you for advice and comforting words. That does not mean to say that we hold their hands and tell them everything, for there would be no point in that, as you all have to learn about life yourselves. But we do have the capability of knowing the future and so will tell them what is essential for them to know for their sakes and so they go forward knowing some help has been given, and that what has been said to them is fact and in truth and love. Their families from the spirit world will have been to speak with them through you with evidence of their survival, sometimes speaking of past events. After this, the people of your world will go away, knowing it all to be true, maybe even the truth has been spoken of the future. I say maybe because, until the future has happened, even though their families from the spirit world can give back-up on evidence, the people on earth expect more, and it is only when what they have been told actually happens that they are a hundred per cent certain and can be expected to believe it as being the truth. We do not mind how long it takes as long as our work helps and convinces the people that there really is a spirit world, and then our job is worthwhile. I believe there is so much help needed on your earth and for centuries, since the earth began, we have been here waiting for people to be aware of our existence and to be recognised. This is now happening and it pleases us very much.

'There are so many people on earth like you, Little One, who have contact with us and understand that I must use you as an instrument for me to be able to carry out my work.'

I understood all this and it made me feel proud to think I could be of some use to the spirit world and very honoured they had chosen me. I had one question I wanted answered so I asked White Arrow, 'Why me, White Arrow? Surely it would have been better to choose someone who had lived a better life and had not done the many wrong things I have done.'

'Why, Little One, should I not want you? If you had not had the path you have followed in life you would not have been any good in the work I must do, for at least you will understand the people and will not judge them because you have shared their experiences. Surely, that is why you have been chosen.' White Arrow said no more on the subject and left.

I was still a bit nervous, thinking I would have to see strangers in my own home, but as White Arrow had not told me exactly when this was to happen I put it out of my mind and life carried on as normal. My family life was a lot happier, thanks to White Arrow.

One night I went to see Mum and the girls and as we sat in the kitchen I said, 'Guess what, Mum, White Arrow wants me to work with him to help other people.'

Mum looked at me and said, 'Don't you think you should, after all he has done for you?'

'Oh, I will,' I said. 'It's just that I'm a bit nervous about it.'

'You'll be OK, love,' she said and I could see the look of pride in her eyes. At long last her wish had come true, her daughter was now cured and looking forward to the future, and also she was well enough and trusted enough to work with the spirit world. I loved her so much and thanked White Arrow for giving her back her real daughter, and prayed that in the years to come I could repay some of the happiness she deserved. She had devoted her life to me and my children and had not had much out of life herself except our love, and I wanted her to have so much more. I remembered what White Arrow had told me about choosing our lives and, as I looked at her, I was sure I had chosen her as my mother. Mum was a bit on the plumpish side and wasn't very tall, being only 5ft 1in. Her hair was slightly tinted and the light that shone through the kitchen window highlighted the red in her hair. She had been a very attractive woman in her younger years. Now she was sixty and the years had taken their toll. She always put everyone before herself. Everybody liked Mum. She was the type of person who would say hello to everyone and smile, even when there were times she didn't feel like it. On the other hand you could only push Mum so far because, for all her tolerance, there were times when she would lose her temper, but she soon calmed down again and would forget all about it straight away. I thought to myself as I sat admiring her, You just don't know how much I love you.

There was a knock at the door. It was Tony. 'I'd better go, Mum,' I said, giving her a kiss on the cheek. 'I'll see you tomorrow night.'

'OK, love,' said Mum, and as I went I popped into the living room to the kids. They were watching television so I called out that I was off home and that I would see them the following evening.

'OK,' they both said, without taking their eyes off the television set – typical of kids, I thought, but I loved them and didn't mind.

Nothing more was said about my working with people for a couple of months, so I carried on learning all I could with White Arrow and the spirit people until one day, right out of the blue, a strange thing happened. We were going along in the car when suddenly a little boy sat on my lap. Instinctively, I knew he was my son and didn't even have to ask White Arrow for confirmation. Although I hadn't completely forgotten the abortion I had had, I had put it at the back of my mind and this was the very first time I had any contact with my child. Until now, I hadn't known whether it was a boy or a girl I had been carrying, and now, here was my son. I was unaware that babies and children grow up in the spirit world. My boy was now sitting on my lap with his arms around my neck and, without thinking, I went to give him a kiss but just in time I stopped myself and remembered that, although the spirit world can cuddle us, we cannot reciprocate because their bodies are not solid. I felt very emotional and before speaking to Tony about his son I turned to White Arrow. I said, 'Does he hate me for getting rid of him?'

White Arrow's reply came softly, 'Little One, look at your

son. Does he not show how much he loves you? Even at his tender age he is much wiser than you for he now knows it was his fate. He chose to be with you for that short time and he chose you to be his mother.'

'Will this be the only time I will be able to see him and be as close to him, White Arrow?' I was impelled to ask.

'No,' he replied. 'You will see your son many times during the course of your lifetime for he will stay with you till the day you die, but he will continue to grow up in spirit and learn. We have many schools here and there are many things for the children to learn, but in between he will visit you occasionally. Remember, God takes nothing away from us.'

My little son was now playing and I turned to Tony. This time, I spoke softly and carefully to Tony. 'Tony, your son is here.'

'Sorry, love, I didn't hear what you said,' said Tony.

This time I spoke louder. 'Your son is sitting on my lap. You know, the baby we had aborted. It was a boy and he's sitting here,' I patted my lap to indicate where our son was sitting.

Tony said nothing but found a place to park the car. When we had stopped he turned to face me and, not doubting me, he said, 'Is he really here?'

I nodded.

Tony said, 'I'm happy he's around, Ann, but it really hurts me that we had to agree to the abortion.' Tony was very remorseful so I tried to cheer him by saying, 'Tony, that's all in the past, my love. What counts is he's here with us.' I went on to explain what White Arrow had said about babies growing up in the spirit world and that seemed to satisfy Tony.

All of a sudden our son went, so I told Tony and said not to worry for we would see him again. The ride home was quiet, as both of us were deep in our own thoughts, but nevertheless pleased with our son's appearance.

One evening, as we sat watching television, the telephone rang. Tony got up to answer it and said it was for me. It was one of my friends on the line who asked if I would do her a favour. She said she had a friend who had many problems and she suggested that I might see her to try to help her. Without thinking, I said yes, and arranged a day for her to come round. My friend thanked me and rang off. Tony asked what my friend wanted so I told him I had agreed to see her friend in order to help her through with White Arrow's guidance. Just then, the penny dropped, and I said, 'God, Tony. I've just realised I'm seeing someone I don't know.'

'Don't panic,' said Tony, and asked me when I had told her I'd see her. I said that it wasn't till the weekend but I thought I'll kill White Arrow! He could have warned me in advance that this was going to happen! I still didn't think I was ready to see strangers yet.

'Yes, Ann,' said Tony. 'But have you considered White Arrow might think you're ready?'

I nodded and said that I hoped so. It seemed daft to worry about it now, it wasn't so much regarding White Arrow, because I was aware of his capabilities – no, it was me. I had worked with people all my life in ordinary jobs but this was something entirely different.

I still had a couple of days to go before my first sitter was due to come and that night I lay awake, thinking it over in my mind. Every time I wanted to have a go at White Arrow he conveniently vanished! The following morning he appeared again and straight away I said to him, 'You could have warned me.'

'What was the point?' White Arrow replied. 'If I had told you weeks ago you would have still been in the same state you are in now, only for longer, so it was better I said nothing.'

I thought about it for a moment then said, 'Yes, you're right. You did tell me I had to work for you.'

He smiled and said, 'Don't be nervous, Little One, leave it all to me.'

'I will!' I replied, trying to act sure of myself, but still thinking I would have to see her in a few days' time.

When the day came I was a bag of nerves. Would she like me? Would she be happy with what White Arrow told her? So many questions and anxieties were going through my mind that by the time she arrived I was totally exhausted from worrying about it. Tony answered the door and showed her in. I was upstairs at the time and Tony came up to tell me she was downstairs. He asked me if I wanted a cup of tea. I said, 'Yes, please, love, and would you also make one for the lady?'

As I walked down the stairs I kept saying over and over to myself, 'Don't let White Arrow down. Try to relax,' but by the time I had got to the door of the room where the lady was, my insides were turning over. I managed to say 'Hello' and sat down. Before I realised it I was explaining to her how I worked, but I should have said it was coming directly from White Arrow for it was as if I had been seeing people all my life. The words just flowed and I was becoming more relaxed as we went along. The woman accepted ninety per cent of what White Arrow was telling her and when we had finished I asked her if she was satisfied with the sitting.

She said, 'Yes, very. You've taken a weight off my shoulders. I didn't know which way to turn and now everything is clear to me.'

As I got up I said, 'Please, do let me know how you get on, I'd be very interested to know.'

With that I showed her to the door and as I walked into the front room my face was beaming.

'I know it went well by the look on your face,' said Tony.

I said how marvellous White Arrow had been and I couldn't understand why I had been so worried. Tony looked at me and said, 'I'm proud of you, Ann.' When I asked him why, he went on, 'Well, because you could have refused to see the lady but you didn't, you trusted White Arrow.'

From that day gradually I began seeing more people and really loving my work. Not only was I making new friends in the living, but also new friends in the spirit world. I felt that White Arrow and I were becoming even closer, if that was possible as we were close anyway, and life was taking on a fresh meaning to me. I felt lucky to be alive and cured, my family were happier, I had White Arrow, and above all

I was now helping other people. Many times I had thanked White Arrow for what he had done for me and I knew in my heart there would be many more thank yous I would owe to him. Most of all I was delighted to think Mum and Tony were proud of me.

Although people were coming and going at our house, life continued much the same as usual. Probably because White Arrow had learned to speak English from watching the television, he was now showing more and more interest in it. He would often pop in and sit with us if there was a programme he particularly wanted to watch. I had got used to all this by now and White Arrow would just plonk himself down anywhere on the floor, as long as he had a good view of the set. He still wasn't used to using furniture and, although we were sitting on chairs, he still persisted in sitting on the floor. That is, unless he was in the bedroom which was the only place he would sit on something or else lie down. I had been watching a film for about half an hour when I looked to see if White Arrow was still there. Yes, there he was, sitting in the same place, when all of a sudden I felt the presence of more spirit people in the room. I looked behind me towards the settee, and sure enough, I was right. Sitting completely absorbed in the film were two people. At first, I thought I was seeing things and I looked over to White Arrow and said mentally, 'Who are your friends?' I thought to myself, Bloomin' cheek. They'll be wanting tea and biscuits next!

Once again, I had forgotten White Arrow can read my mind and I heard him say, in a deadpan face, 'No sugar!'

'Hah! Very funny, White Arrow.'

I looked over at White Arrow and wondered about my future. At least with him with me I was certain I would never get bored! Just then, he turned and looked at me. Trying not to laugh, I said, 'Are you really sure I chose my own life, and that I chose you to come back as my guide?'

He didn't say a word but just gave me one of those looks and turned his head back to the television set. I felt smug because he couldn't think of a witty enough answer.

White Arrow told me what the future had in store for me,

and one of the things he mentioned was that I would have a car. I had never owned a car of my own before because Tony had always had one, so I was really excited at the prospect of owning my very own.

Time went by and after another six months I was still waiting for this car to come my way and I was getting a little impatient. I sat waiting for it to arrive on my doorstep, then one morning, as I sat in the living room, I suddenly realised there was no point in my having a car when I couldn't drive and didn't even own a licence. White Arrow nodded his head in acknowledgement.

He said, 'That's right, what's the point in giving you a car when you can't drive? I can't give you the certificate to say you have passed your driving test, that is impossible, so you must go for it yourself. Whatever we give you from the spirit world you must give fifty per cent yourself, otherwise there would be no point in it if everything came that easily. You have to meet us half-way and show you can earn it, for you would do nothing to help yourself and wouldn't appreciate anything if it was given to you on a plate.'

I understood him, so the following week I booked my driving lessons. All went well, so when my driving test was coming up I asked White Arrow if I would pass or not.

He said, 'Yes,' but no more than that, so I was really pleased.

I thought no more about it until the day before, when I was walking round to see Mum and the girls. Suddenly White Arrow told me I would fail. I was so angry with him and said, 'Thanks a lot! Why wait until now to tell me?'

He replied, 'Tomorrow you will be too sure of yourself and that is why you will fail. I said Yes, you would pass initially, but I didn't necessarily mean it would be tomorrow's test and now you know the reason why.'

'Rubbish!' I retorted. Although I was nervous about the driving test, the following day I felt very confident and capable of passing it, so I made up my mind to ignore what he had said.

Mum asked me how I was feeling about the test so I told

her that White Arrow said I would fail, but I was sure I would pass.

Mum laughed and said, 'Well, Ann, I sincerely hope you're right, but don't be too disappointed if you don't. Remember, you always say White Arrow is always right, so keep an open mind and see what happens.'

I thanked Mum for her kind words, for I knew White Arrow meant well and didn't want to see me upset if I did fail, and that in her heart, Mum hoped I would pass first time.

The following morning I woke bright and early. I cannot truthfully say I had no butterflies in my stomach, but I was raring to go. My driving instructor picked me up and in the lesson before the test everything went well.

I can remember saying to myself, You're wrong, White Arrow. This time I'll prove it, and this time *I* am right, and not you!

Throughout the one hour lesson before the test, White Arrow sat in the back of the car. I tried to ignore him, because I felt I had to make it on my own.

When we arrived at the driving test centre, he vanished, then, but it didn't really concern me, all I cared about was getting it over and done with. When the examiner walked me to the car I was shaking like a jelly, but after a few minutes I calmed myself down. I whispered under my breath to White Arrow that I was going to pass easily. Everything went fine until I had to reverse round a corner. When the examiner told me to make this manoeuvre I got a bit too confident, and I went up the kerb for what seemed a mile! I knew then that I had failed and that White Arrow was correct in his prediction. I will not write down the exact words that came into my head at that precise moment, but the poor examiner was getting panicky and must have thought to himself, Whenever is she going to stop? I went to pieces and, for some unknown reason, let go of the wheel, put my foot down hard on the brake so that by the time the car had ground to a halt with a jerk, the car was facing out on to the road with the back wheels completely up the curb and on the pavement. How embarrassing!

'Er, shall we carry on?' said the examiner sarcastically, as he rearranged his now hot and sticky collar. I was so eager to get back to the centre, if only to have a go at White Arrow. When we pulled up the examiner said, 'Mrs Walker, you have failed.'

I had calmed down somewhat by the time I reached home. White Arrow was sitting on the floor when I went indoors and I said. 'Don't bother to tell me I told you so! In future, don't tell me whether I will pass or not.'

To put it mildly, I was not in the best of moods. White Arrow told me to put in for another test straight away and that I would pass it this time. 'You have now learnt your lesson not to be sure of yourself.'

I considered this criticism for a moment and unfortunately had to agree with him. Yes, I had been too confident this morning and it was completely my own fault. I had taken the reverse round the corner far too quickly, thinking I could handle it. I looked at White Arrow and said, 'Your trouble is, you know too much!'

'That's my job,' he replied nonchalantly.

I passed next time with flying colours. It was the first time I had actually achieved something by myself apart from coming off the pills. I was highly delighted and pleased with myself and everyone, including White Arrow, congratulated me. I was so excited that I completely forgot that now I had a full driving licence I could get my very own car.

White Arrow has always said that you can count the number of very close friends we have on one hand and at the time I had three such friends. They were Jean and a couple named Bill and Isobel. All three of them had always taken me for good or bad and if ever I needed help they were first there. I told Jean I had passed my test and two days later she telephoned me to ask me if I wanted a car. I was a bit surprised and said I would love one but I couldn't afford one at the moment. Jean went on to say she knew someone who had a car for sale who would be only too willing for me to pay monthly. It was only £500 and I reckoned I could afford to pay by instalments. I told Jean I would love it and she told me to see her on Sunday to go and have a look at the car. She guaranteed I'd like it. That night I went to bed so excited and as I lay there I asked White Arrow if this was the right car for me that he'd promised I'd have. To my amazement he replied, 'No, Ann, you can't have this one.'

For a moment I thought, No, I'm not hearing this, and looked up at White Arrow in disbelief. He continued, 'Sincerely, this is not the car for you, it is not the one I promised.'

'Well, White Arrow,' I said haughtily, 'I don't care what you think. I'm having this car. All my life I've wanted one and now's my chance,' and with that I turned over and went to sleep, having made up my mind I would have it whether he said yes or no.

I could hardly wait for Sunday to arrive. I went along with Jean to look at the car and, without hesitation, agreed to buy it. I drove it home, having made insurance arrangements the previous day as I was so sure about getting it. I showed it to Mum and Tony and the children. I felt so proud of myself to be capable, for once in my life, of doing anything like this on my own. I thought to myself, There you are, White Arrow, I've got the car. By the end of the month I had not earned enough to pay the monthly instalment and so I had to sell it. The car cost me £500 and I reluctantly sold it for £200. The ironic thing here is that a few months after I'd sold it I could have afforded to pay for it, but White Arrow had always been determined I wasn't to have this car from the very beginning. I decided to take notice of him, and learnt yet another lesson the hard way. It wasn't that White Arrow was trying to run my life for me, but he was trying to tell me that at that particular time I could not possibly afford it. In a short time I bought another car and this time I was able to pay for it without any problem.

White Arrow told me of many events that were to occur in my lifetime, some of which were more important than others. They were not everyday events because that is not spirits' way, but what he told me had pleased me. Sometimes the good things he told me would happen seemed impossible but

I trusted his word and never questioned him and accepted it to be fact. Something was about to happen, however, which he omitted to tell me about, something I would never have expected to ever happen to me, and perhaps this is why White Arrow didn't mention it, for fear that I would not believe him. Or was it that I didn't want to believe it, for it was something that was to hurt me for ever. One Saturday morning, my daughter and I set off down the road to do some shopping. As we passed the Post Office I stopped and said to Joyce that I was going to put £1 into a Post Office Savings Account. I had no intention of doing so beforehand but felt impelled to do so at this time. When White Arrow had told me my future some time ago, he told me I would one day go to the United States. When he told me this I thought, Yes, and pigs can fly, for at that time there was no way I could ever possibly even consider taking a holiday in America. As we came out of the Post Office I told Joyce that the following year I was going to take them all to America. She looked at me as if I was crazy but said that she hoped so. I said we would definitely go without being able to imagine how the hell I would be able to raise enough money. I had opened the account in the hope that it wouldn't all be just a daydream of mine for I so wanted Mum to have a holiday of a lifetime as well as the children. I knew Tony wouldn't fly as he hates the idea, and I also knew he would hate me to go on holiday without him, so I said nothing about it to him.

I saved so hard during the months that followed and each night I prayed I would make it. It was as if there was something or someone pushing me to work hard for this holiday. Whenever I asked White Arrow if I would be able to get them all to America he would just smile and nod his head.

'Little One,' he said, 'you'll make it, for it is in your destiny.'

'But will I make it now?' I asked. He didn't answer me, but just smiled.

The money was growing and by hard work I knew I could

do it. During this period my aunt would come round to see my Mum. Mum would revel in showing Aunt Doris my savings book and would say to her over a cup of tea, 'Look we're what Ann has saved. We're going to America.'

Doris asked Mum when she thought we might go. I had been saving hard for four months by now and Mum told Doris we would be going this year. She so looked forward to going and had trusted me to carry it out. I knew my mother wanted to prove to everyone that at long last we could do the things other families do. I loved her for the faith she had in me after all these years, and that made me more determined to get her there.

My eldest daughter's twenty-first birthday was coming up in the July and she begged me to throw a big party for her. We had only managed very small birthday parties up until now but, as Mum had a quiet word with me to see if we could afford a big celebration for her, even if it meant forgoing the holiday, I had to agree. After all, she was more important than a holiday, but I was sure we could manage. How lucky my kids were to have such a wonderful woman for their grandmother. Here was a woman who had never been abroad, with the possibility of the holiday of a lifetime, yet she was willing to give it all up for her granddaughter. This made me appreciate her and love her all the more and made me more determined to take her away to America. I was also determined my daughter would have a party she would never forget, so with a limited amount of money it was possible to go ahead with the party plans. I hired a large hall at the Civic Centre a couple of weeks after Mum had spoken to me about it.

Chapter 17

It was now March. I carried on saving for the holiday. One Sunday I went to church with Tony, and as the service started I sat there quietly with my eyes shut. Suddenly I saw a vision. I could see my mother was dead and the fear that was in my heart was almost too much to bear. I wanted to rush out of the church there and then to make sure she was all right, but I knew I couldn't in front of all these people.

As I sat there, praying for the service to finish quickly so that I could rush home to see Mum, another vision appeared. This time it was my Uncle Bill who was dying. I know it sounds dreadful but I felt relief and thought, It's all right, it's not Mum after all. I had made a mistake, it was Uncle Bill. As soon as the service had finished I still felt eager to rush round to Mum's to check on her. I knocked on the door and Mum called out, 'Who is it?' Mum never did answer the door without knowing who it was first. As she opened the door to me I felt such relief.

'Hello, Mum, are you all right?' I asked.

'Of course I am,' she replied, wondering why I had an anxious tone in my voice. I kissed her on the cheek. I didn't even tell Tony. I thought it was my imagination playing tricks on me.

It was almost July and I had managed to book our holiday. Tony said he didn't mind not going. I had asked him, of course, but he wouldn't come, while Karen said if I didn't mind she'd rather go somewhere else with her friend. I can't pretend I wasn't disappointed because I had really hoped all the family would come with me and now it was just myself, Mum and Joyce.

It was two weeks before the party when I had a dream that my cousin and grandmother were both in spirit and they were at Karen's party. They were sitting at a table reading a will. I could not understand, but took it that Karen was about to depart from this world. It was a horrible dream and in it I was crying and yet the party carried on.

The following morning I was so upset when I awoke that I had to have a word with White Arrow about my terrible dream. I asked him if anything was wrong, but he said nothing, so I presumed there was nothing to worry about or surely he would have warned me?

The party went really well with lots of laughter and fun. All the family came along with Karen's friends. She was thrilled and thoroughly enjoyed herself.

We were due to fly out a fortnight after the party, one year almost to the day that I had put the first pound into the Post Office. I think White Arrow had performed a miracle because I had never achieved so much in my lifetime as I had in the past twelve months. Mum had never flown before and was getting really excited about the prospect of going overseas. Joyce had a boyfriend by this time but was also looking forward to the holiday as she had never been abroad either. I also decided to ask my friend Jean. We were to fly out on the Monday and at the airport I kissed Tony goodbye, promising to ring him when we arrived at the hotel.

Typical of my luck, when we arrived at the first hotel we were booked into it turned out not to be up to standard, but, luckily, Jean managed to change hotels.

The very first day I fell asleep on the beach. Having lain in the sun too long I got badly sunburnt. I felt very ill that night but didn't want to spoil anyone's fun, so the following day I agreed to go to the beach again, provided I could use a canopy which would keep me in the shade. My daughter and my friend went for a walk whilst I stayed talking to Mum. They returned half an hour later, having arranged to go on a boat trip, and came back to ask us if we would be interested in going, too. I was beginning to feel a lot better despite the fact that the temperature was in the nineties. I asked Mum if she wanted to go, but she said she'd prefer to stay in her hotel room and watch television where it would be cooler.

We walked Mum back to the hotel and got changed for the

boat trip, which was going to somewhere called Shell Island. We all climbed on board with me wearing Mum's hat and Jean's shawl round my shoulders, and I sat back to enjoy the trip. I thought back to White Arrow once telling me I would one day go on a catamaran so I looked up and to my surprise realised the boat was indeed a catamaran. Well done White Arrow! I said in my mind, and then it dawned on me that I hadn't seen him since we had arrived and asked, 'Where are you?' I got no reply so just carried on enjoying myself.

As the boat approached the island I made up my mind I would be the very first to jump off the boat. So, with my hat on my head, and the shawl still around my shoulders, I jumped as we touched the shore. The next thing I knew I was going down, down and down. The hat went one way, the shawl the other, and there seemed to be no bottom to the water. I was sinking deeper and I said to myself, 'Here we go again, Ann. It could only happen to you!' It was a good job I am a good swimmer, for as soon as I decided I had gone down far enough I swam back up.

Gasping for breath, I managed to crawl on to the sands. Everyone was laughing at me. As I lay there I thought, Don't give up, Ann, you've another twelve days to go yet. It's got to get better!

In the end, despite all our mishaps, we had a fantastic time. It had been a wonderful, new experience for us all and we all looked so well on our return. We came back at the end of August which, so far, had been a good year for us all. White Arrow had made a few appearances on holiday but had only stayed a very short time, so I had not seen that much of him and missed him as much as Tony. Our holiday meant so much to all of us and I was only too grateful to have been able to take Mum and Joyce with me. I had never had so much fun in my whole life, and I know the same applied to them, too, as well as my friend Jean.

It is amazing how very quickly life returns to the old familiar routine. We were in September by now and it turned out not to be a very good month for us. Joyce broke up with her boyfriend, Karen had to go into hospital for a minor operation, and Mum was not well. I wondered at first if the heat had been too much for her when we were on holiday, or perhaps the travelling had upset her system.

By the end of September the girls had managed to sort themselves out, but Mum was still not well. She went to the doctor as she was having pain in her shoulder, near her chest. The doctor sent her to have an X-ray. I had been continuing my work with White Arrow as before, but had noticed he wasn't his usual self. He was very quiet in between clients. I was more concerned about Mum, through, and not once did I consider asking White Arrow what the matter was with Mum. On reflection, this was odd, as I had always turned to him for advice and guidance.

Mum was due for a hospital visit on the Thursday and that morning my mind went back to before the holiday. I had forgotten so many things which had been told to me by the spirit world, only to remember when it seemed important – and I was remembering now. Tony was home that morning and as I sat down reflecting on the things I had been shown and told, I felt just as if *I* had cancer. Frightened, I said to Tony, 'I think I'm going to die of cancer, you know.'

'Good God,' said Tony. 'What on earth makes you say that?'

'I don't know. I keep feeling I've got cancer.' I was well aware I was frightening him and tried to lighten the atmosphere by saying, 'Don't worry, love, maybe I'm picking up someone else's condition and it isn't me after all.'

The memory came back of the bad dream I had had back in July and then it made me rethink. Not Mum, surely not, not my Mum? I was saying it over and over in my head in disbelief. I didn't want to ask White Arrow for fear he would tell me it was true. I tried to convince myself that I was over-reacting, after all, she's only got a pain in her shoulder and chest. Surely you can't have cancer in the shoulder. I was hoping that after the X-ray I would be able to relax a little. No news came from the hospital for about a week, but I was worried about Mum as she was not looking at all well, and I was very annoyed with the hospital staff for not letting us know sooner.

Then one morning Mum phoned me to say she had received a letter from the hospital and they wanted to see her again for another X-ray. Mum must have sensed my concern because she told me not to worry: maybe the first X-ray didn't come out properly. I hoped to God she was right. She said she had an appointment for the following Thursday so I said to try not to think about it and that I was sure all would be OK. 'I'll see you later, but please stop worrying, Mum,' and she said she would do her best.

After I put the phone down I sat there, thinking about how much she meant to me. I had to speak to White Arrow about it so I said to him, 'White Arrow, I'm so scared about losing Mum. Please, don't let anything happen to her.'

'Little One, I am here. I will give you all the strength you need,' he said, but nothing more, and sat next to me. I kept going over in my mind how much that wonderful woman had done for me all those years. She had brought me into the world, fed and clothed me, and loved me all that time, not once complaining about the trouble I had given her. I was filled with fear that morning and, turning to look at White Arrow, said with tears in my eyes, 'If anything, White Arrow, I would even go without you rather than anything happen to Mum, for she is my life. I owe her so much and I need time to repay her. Please, give me that chance.' For the first time, I saw tears in White Arrow's eyes, which really upset me all the more. He had never before cried in front of me and as he put his arms round me he said gently, 'Little One, what is to be, will be, but I promise you your mother will never leave you.'

Perhaps I shouldn't have said what I did, but at that stage I was clutching at straws, holding on to anything that would allow me to keep my mother.

As the dreaded Thursday appointment drew nearer I could take no more of it, and it wasn't fair on White Arrow to ask him any more on the subject. In the past few days he had been like my shadow, following me everywhere. Mum's appointment at the hospital was in the afternoon, and it had been arranged that Aunty Doris would take Mum and pick me up on the way there. Before they arrived I decided to telephone my medium friend, Derek, to ask him what was wrong with Mum. Within seconds there was an immense power circulating around me, a power full of strength and love way beyond my wildest dreams. It was almost overpowering me and then I heard Derek talking to his guide. He came back to say, 'Ann, I'm sorry, but as I understand it, your Mum has cancer.'

All I could think of to say was, 'Thanks, Derek, for your help,' and I put the receiver down. I kept repeating that horrid word over and over. Should I tell my aunt my fears? I never doubted the spirit world so I thought, No, let's wait and see what the hospital says. I looked at White Arrow and the same unbelievable strength was around me. He was still so close to me and I decided that I wouldn't ask just yet. I'd wait for Mum to come home first and see what happened then.

We went to the hospital and they took another X-ray. To my amazement everything was clear. I was relieved and delighted with the result and so glad I hadn't told Aunt what Derek had said. When I got back home I couldn't wait for Tony to come in. As soon as he got in the front door he asked how Mum was.

'Fine!' I said. 'So what do you think about Derek telling me Mum has cancer?'

'Ann, I really don't know what to think. Does White Arrow say nothing at all about it?' Tony asked.

I replied, 'Well, he still seems so unhappy and not his usual self at all, which worries me.'

Tony said, 'Do you think he's not telling you everything?'

'No. He told me Mum was going to be with me always, so it can't be that bad.'

Tony kissed me and told me to try not to worry. He suggested we go by the hospital results and accept that the news was good after all. It was the middle of October by now and Mum was getting no better. The pain in her shoulder was still there and now she was suffering pain in her stomach. Once again the doctor sent her for an X-ray, this time for her stomach. I was beside myself with worry since the pain in her stomach had started, but still White Arrow was saying nothing about it.

One morning I said to Tony, 'Tony, I've had enough. I'm going to see Mum's doctor because she is in so much pain all the time and yet nothing seems to be done about it.' Tony agreed with me and made the appointment for me for that evening. I didn't tell Mum I was going when I spoke to her on the phone earlier in the day.

The doctor seemed a very pleasant man. I was taken with his soft and caring voice. I had to remind myself that I was there to talk about Mum and not to dwell on how nice her doctor was. Inside my head I was asking, 'Where are you, White Arrow? I need you.' Then he appeared. He put his hand on my shoulder, which calmed me a little, and I proceeded to tell the doctor my worries about Mum.

'Mrs Walker,' the doctor replied, 'I would not like you to repeat to anyone what I am about to tell you, but the hospital thinks your mother has a tumour in her stomach. We cannot be certain how serious it is until we have carried out more tests.'

'Thank you,' I said, mostly for his honesty and, as there was nothing else to say, I left. As I was walking to the car I thought, Well, they can remove a tumour so there's hope yet, but somehow, deep down, I knew I was kidding myself. It was almost as if I was being prepared without realising it. God knew how I loved that woman and that night when I went to see her there was pain in my heart. Once again, I said to White Arrow, 'Don't let anything happen to her.' His reply was what he had told me before, 'You'll never lose her, Little One.'

I understood it, to mean as I had the first time he told me, that she was going to pull through and that everything would be all right. However, I felt I couldn't take all the responsibility of knowing she was ill by myself, so Tony suggested I contact my brother and tell him, as he had the right to know. My brother has three daughters, one of whom like her father, is deaf and dumb. When I telephoned him the middle one answered. 'Could you tell Daddy I want to see him tonight, darling?' She went away to speak to Raymond and when she came back she said, 'Daddy is coming over now.'

Before Raymond arrived Mum phoned me to ask me to go round to see her for a little while because she wasn't feeling at all well.

I said I couldn't possibly make it for about an hour and made up some excuse about having someone coming to see me, but really it was because I had to be home for Raymond when he arrived, and didn't want Mum to know he was coming. Mum said, 'OK, but try not to be too long, will you, love.'

As I rang off I started panicking because it was so unlike Mum to call me so late in the day. It was already about nine o'clock when Ray arrived and I explained to him as quickly as possible what the doctor had told me and that Mum had been on the phone complaining of not feeling well. We both went round and stayed with Mum till my girls came in.

The following morning I was not coping with the situation at all well. Although White Arrow was still with me for my clients I felt the need to visit my doctor. I related my predicament and very reluctantly he put me back on drugs, prescribing five Valium a day.

The Valium took the edge off to start with, but Mum took a turn for the worse later that week and was due for a check-up at the hospital on the following Monday. When the doctor saw her he decided she was too ill to go home; they would keep her in hospital in order to do tests straight away.

I went to the hospital half an hour before visiting time so I could have a word with the doctor. Tony stayed outside, knowing I wanted to be on my own with the doctor. I walked into the sister's office and the doctor was in there talking to her. 'Can I have a word with you please, Doctor?' I said, and explained who I was. He was very kind and agreed to speak with me. The sister left so that we could speak privately and the doctor told me about Mum's problem. At first he hesitated so I told him I wanted to know the truth. Mum lay in her hospital bed, unaware I was there and with the doctor.

I thought to myself, Please hurry, we've only thirty minutes to discuss my mother's future before visitors are permitted and if I'm not with Mum at three o'clock on the dot she'll worry. Although I told him I wanted the truth, deep in my heart I didn't want to know it.

The doctor then told me Mum had cancer of the liver. I knew he couldn't have made a mistake, as he had the results of her tests in his hands.

There I was, standing on my own for the very first time in my life, with no mother to support me. My first thought was, 'God damn him,' and yet it wasn't his fault, poor man. I had asked him for the truth and that's what he told me. My mind was divided – half was on the doctor, the other with my mother whose bed I could see down the middle of the ward. It could have only been a matter of seconds but, even so, a million and one questions entered my head. How do I tell the kids? How do I tell Tony and Raymond? How on earth would I be able to cope without her?

I realised I hadn't asked him how long Mum had to live. He said she had three months to a year, that was all. Once again I took the optimistic approach, well, a year, if only they could keep her alive for a year, maybe . . . my heart started to jump, maybe there was a glimmer of hope, that she may be able to live a long time yet, maybe . . . lots of maybes came into my mind. I didn't want to believe it, but the worst was yet to come. I knew I had to go home to tell my children their grandmother was terminally ill. She was the one woman who had kept us all together.

The doctor went on to tell me what tests they had carried out on Mum, then I told him what Mum's own GP had told me in confidence. Whether it was the Valium or White Arrow's influence, I don't know, but any other time I wouldn't have been able to ask for the truth, let alone hear and accept it.

By the time I got to Tony I was crying uncontrollably. The

tears were flowing down my face and I said, 'Oh, Tony, she's dying. What do I do now?'

I kept sobbing when, suddenly, another arm was around me. It was my aunt, who had come up to see Mum with my uncle. I told her what the doctor had said and started to wipe my tears away as visitors were now arriving. I didn't want Mum to see my tears and how I kept them at bay I will never know. As I walked up towards Mum's bed I smiled at her and said, 'Doris and Eddie are here, Mum, so I won't stay long but I'll be up again tonight, all right?' To be honest, I couldn't get away quickly enough, for that was one of the hardest things I have ever had to do.

I cried all the way home and by the time I reached home the pain inside me was intolerable. Why her, God? Anyone else, but not her. All her life she has given her love to us and now she was dying. Now He was going to take her.

'It's just isn't fair, it just isn't fair,' I screamed.

'Come on, love,' Tony said. 'Try and pull yourself together. The kids have got to know and you're the one who'll have to tell them. It'll come better from you.'

I told Tony I would have to take a Valium tablet if I was to tell them right now. My intake of pills had doubled but I knew I couldn't cope without them. Tony was getting worried about this, I knew, but he didn't say anything about it. Without them I wouldn't be able to cope at all and I had to do that for Mum's sake and the children.

Karen was in that afternoon and so I saw her first, and when we picked up Joyce from work I told her too about their grandmother. Both were in tears. I knew they hadn't taken it all in, as I hadn't when I was first told, and their first reaction was to rush to the hospital to see her. It was too early for her to receive visitors so we all sat around and waited for an hour and a half to pass before we would be allowed in. It seemed we were sitting there for a lifetime, with hardly a word exchanged between us. There was still my brother to tell, but I thought I'd leave it till I had seen Mum, then get him to come over to see me.

The girls and I were all wearing heavy make-up to hide

our red eyes and when we were permitted to go into the ward the girls sat one either side of her bed. I felt so proud of them because they put on a brave face, laughing and smiling, yet they must have felt wretched inside. Now and again they would pop outside to have a weep and then compose themselves once more before going back to see her.

When it was time for us to leave we kissed Mum in turn, trying not to let her know anything was amiss, almost as if we were playing a cheating game. All the way home we were silent, each wrapped up in our own private thoughts. All our hearts weighed heavy in the knowledge we would soon be losing her. I managed to get in touch with Raymond, which was always difficult, his being deaf and dumb. He couldn't express himself as clearly as we could and as I told him the sad news he just sat there and cried, 'I love her.' We cuddled each other for a while, realising no words were needed to express our combined emotions.

When Raymond left he said he would meet me at the hospital the next day.

The following week I asked the doctor at the hospital if it was at all possible for us to take Mum home. He agreed because he said there was nothing more they could do for her. We picked her up on the Friday and I am not sure if Mum knew in her heart that she was going to die, but she dreaded the thought of going home. Perhaps she had put two and two together, realising the hospital were unable to do any more for her. I had asked the doctors not to tell Mum their diagnosis and they kept their promise.

We all took shifts to look after Mum. We brought the bed down into the back room for her. My family felt it better for me to continue seeing clients as normal as this might prevent my mother from thinking there was something wrong, and so I took the night shift. I used to sleep in the same room as her and then, in the morning, we would do everything that was necessary and then both my daughters took over in the afternoon and evening. My mother never really believed in spirit, as I have mentioned before, but one night, right out of the blue, I remember saying to her, 'Can I put my hands on your shoulder, Mum?' She was in terrible pain from the cancer. I had always believed one was either directed to be a medium or a healer, never both. But I put my hands on her shoulder and gave her spiritual healing for the very first time. A couple of nights later I asked Mum how the pain was and she said that the only time she had relief from it was when I had laid my hands on her. I will never forget that.

My Mum's sister and my grandfather, who are both in spirit, had been very much around for a couple of days and one evening, because it was such a warm evening, I had the back door open. My mother said to me, 'There's a man at the door, Ann. I can see him.'

'That's all right, Mum,' I said, 'I'll show him out into the back garden and then I'll shut the door.' It was of course my grandfather and I knew she had seen him. He had come for her to help her pass to spirit. Everything is to do with fate. I would never allow the nurses to be with my mother at night because I wanted to look after her at night time. However, the nurses who had been coming round since Mum had been back home told me that I must have a night off because I was getting so tired, and that if I didn't get my rest I would be no good to anybody.

At first I argued with them, but they were so insistent that I agreed to take the night off. My God, am I glad I did. I slept on the sofa and the night nurse sat up all night with my mother until she woke me up at 5 a.m. to tell me my mother was dying. This gave me time to get my family together. As we gathered round the bed, I looked down at the bottom of the bed, and there stood my mother. However, my grief was so great that I just turned away and looked back at her body lying in the bed. My mother had gone.

As we all left the room, both my girls went into the hall holding each other, crying. Raymond sat on the stairs, crying. I cuddled him and he cuddled me. All of us felt such a great loss. Tony stood in the background, ready to comfort me when I needed him. As I embraced my brother, I looked over his shoulder and up the stairs and there, standing at the top, was my mother once again. In my distress I shut my eyes tight – No, I thought, it can't be possible. I opened my eyes again but this time she had gone.

There were so many things to be done that day and, although I was distraught, strength was coming from somewhere. My brother and I made the funeral arrangements and we stayed till early evening making sure the girls would be all right, then returned home.

During these difficult and testing weeks, White Arrow had been with me throughout, but because I had so much on my mind I had hardly spoken to him. I felt numb all day, an odd sensation as if it wasn't really me. Tony said, 'Would you like a cup of tea, love, or something to eat? I'll tell you what, you go upstairs and rest and I'll bring you up something later.'

He knew I wanted to be left on my own and I thanked him for his understanding and never-ending support. I took his advice and went upstairs and as I climbed into bed I reached for my Bible, which was on the bedside table.

It took me back to the last Christmas when Mum had asked me what I would like as a present from her, and this was the Bible which she had bought me. I have never been a religious person so, to be honest, I was surprised at myself for wanting it, but Mum had said, 'Well, Ann, if that's what you want, I'll get you one.'

As I opened the front of my Bible I saw her words which were written on the inside cover, 'To Ann, Love Mum xxx'. It all came back to me and I remembered only too clearly how I had asked Mum to write in it for me. I looked for a pen and wrote beneath Mum's words, 'Mum passed to spirit. Look after her, God. God Bless her. I will miss her very much.' I clung to the Bible and was so glad I had asked Mum for it. It had been the first time that day that I had been on my own and suddenly it hit me. I sat back, the tears rolling down my cheeks, thinking how we had done everything together, we had been inseparable, so what was I going to do without her? The pain in me was intolerable and I grieved, when all of a sudden White Arrow appeared. I said to him, 'Not now, White Arrow.' I didn't mean to hurt him but I wanted to be left on my own with my thoughts of

Mum, but White Arrow was insistent and said, 'Little One, look up, please.'

My head was in my hands. White Arrow went on, 'I have brought your mother with me to see you as I am looking after her.'

I slowly lifted my head and at first I couldn't see her, only him.

Realising my anticipation, he said, 'She's here, Little One,' then, when I looked again, she was standing next to him. She looked exactly the same as when I saw her that morning, only this time she didn't go but sat down beside me on the bed. I so wanted to hold her and never let her go, but I had already learnt that I couldn't possibly hold her. She held her hand out and laid it on mine and said, 'Don't cry, Ann. I haven't gone away from you, but have come back to you and the girls. Nothing in the world could have stopped me from returning to you and the girls because I love you too much.'

By this time White Arrow had gone, leaving Mum and I to talk alone.

'Why you, Mum, why you? Surely it would have been better for me to have gone instead of you.' I was thinking of the children and the love that they had for Mum. I knew I could never take her place in their eyes or would want to.

'Ann,' Mum replied, 'my time was up but at least you and I are more fortunate than most, for you can still see me and hear me. There are many who can't and it must be more difficult for them to accept.'

I understood what Mum was saying but it didn't ease the pain.

'Mum,' I said, 'I want to join you. I can't carry on and don't want to go on without you. I don't care about my future, just you.'

'Now, don't be daft, Ann,' Mum said. 'Whatever you do in the future be sure I'll always be there with you. Nothing has changed.' I looked at her and knew she was right. After all, wasn't she sitting there next to me with her hand on mine? It still wasn't me same as cuddling her and oh, how I wanted to.

'You must go on,' Mum continued. 'Not only for your sake, but for Tony's and the children's. They all need you now and in the future.'

I just couldn't accept this, for Mum had been the only person who had kept the family together, and without her around I knew it would fall apart.

'Mum,' I said, 'I want to come to you. I want to die . . .' and at this juncture White Arrow appeared. He spoke very quietly, 'Little One, I cannot order you not to take your own life but if you do decide to take it you will not be able to join your mother.'

I hated him for saying that and it made me very angry. 'You promised me I would be able to make it up to Mum for all the wrong doings I had done in the past. You promised me she would always be around, you promised.' I repeated it over and over and getting myself into a terrible state.

White Arrow said, 'Little One, I have kept my promise. She is here.'

'It's not the same,' I replied, sobbing. I tried to make White Arrow see my point of view and at the same time was so glad Mum was here right next to me. I was so confused.

Just then, we heard Tony coming up the stairs. Mum kissed me and said, 'I'll be back, you'll see.' I cried myself to sleep.

Mum's body was taken to the Chapel of Rest. When I was working with the spirit world and White Arrow they managed to take the pain of grief away, but in between clients I had to come back to face reality. I made up my mind to see Mum in the Chapel of Rest and as I stood there looking at her silent, unreal form, standing next to her coffin stood White Arrow and Mum together. As the tears started to flow once more, I begged Mum to go back into her body to come back to the living, but she did not answer me. I turned to White Arrow and begged him on my knees, 'Please, I'll do anything, just bring her back to me.'

I seemed to be kneeling for ever, sobbing my heart out and when I got up I touched Mum. She looked so normal so I stroked her face and hair, still wishing the impossible. I knew

I couldn't stay there much longer as the children wanted to see her to pay their last respects, but at the same time I didn't want to leave her. It was crazy really, for I knew I would be able to see her again the following day.

My intake of Valium had steadily increased to seventeen a day. The funeral was only a few days away and I was dreading it. I had to visit my doctor every other day as he was keeping a close eye on me in case I did anything silly. He didn't want me to attend Mum's funeral because he didn't think I'd be able to cope, but of course I had to go. On one of my visits to him he said to me, 'Ann, surely, as you work with the spirit world, death should not be that important to you as you understand about it all.'

I was taken aback. He didn't seem to realise what a great loss I had suffered and that I was finding it virtually impossible to cope with the knowledge I could never again hold her in my arms in the way I had when she was alive. I said nothing in reply to him – what could I say?

The day of the funeral arrived and, like anyone else who's lost a loved one, I was in a complete daze. I felt as if part of me had died with her. The rest of the family were so good and supportive to the four of us for they knew how much Mum had meant to us all.

That night, when it was all over, I crept into bed, exhausted, and tried to block the day out of my mind. As I drifted off to sleep my last thoughts were that this had been one of the unhappiest days of my life.

My depression began to lift when Mum began to come to me a few days later, and then she was with me most of the time. My anger with White Arrow had almost gone and I felt I owed him an apology.

Mum appeared one evening and sat beside of me. 'Ann,' she said, distinctly, 'promise me you won't take any more Valium. Don't go backwards, love. I don't want to see you ill again.'

'I promised her and the following I went back to see the doctor. He was so pleased I wanted to come off them and agreed to help me. It was difficult, but I started that day and when I got down to ten a day I started to feel ill. I was having shooting pains in my chest and left arm.

I told Tony and he suggested I tell the doctor about it.

'Oh, I'll go in a couple of days, you never know, it might go away,' I said.

'No you won't,' said Tony. 'I'll make you an appointment for today. It can't be right to have pains in your chest and arms, Ann, you know that.'

I knew Tony was right and accepted his advice. The doctor examined me and sent me to the hospital for a check-up.

We had an appointment for the following day. An ECG was carried out by a nurse who explained it all to me afterwards.

'Mrs Walker,' she said, 'I would like you to see the doctor. Can you come back in two hours' time?' What else could I do but agree? So we set off for home only to have to return a little later. Tony looked really worried and said he hoped there was nothing seriously wrong. I told him not to worry and that I was sure I was all right.

When we returned to see the doctor at the hospital he told me he wanted me to go into hospital as I had suffered a slight heart attack. I was panic-stricken, not because of the diagnosis but I could remember Mum being in hospital during her last illness and I couldn't face going in myself just now. I made out that I was experiencing many problems at home and couldn't possibly come in. Tony gave me one of those looks – but he knew it was no use arguing with me once I had made up my mind not to do something.

All he said to me on our way home was, 'Are you feeling all right, Ann?' Other than that he was very quiet and subdued. Then, when we got indoors, he said, 'Ann, please go into hospital and do what they tell you to do. It's for your own good.'

I said, 'Tony, if I went in just now, it would kill me, I can't go, I'm sorry.'

Suddenly White Arrow appeared. I hadn't seen him all day and I was very surprised he hadn't mentioned this little lot to me.

White Arrow had an important message for Tony. He told me he wanted Tony to take me to see a different doctor.

'Fine,' I said, 'but who, and why?'

He told me the name of a doctor I had known years ago.

'He will give you both the answer to your problem, but tell Tony you are definitely not coming to the spirit world yet, for there is still a lot of work for you to do.' I passed on everything White Arrow said, and added that White Arrow had never been wrong before, so we had to trust him.

Tony accepted White Arrow's words for he trusted him implicitly. He seemed a bit brighter to hear this news and said it made him feel a bit better, but we'd have to see what the doctor said about it all.

The following day we made an appointment with the doctor whom White Arrow had suggested we consult. I went privately so that I could have check-ups without going into hospital, and this had been White Arrow's plan all along.

After all the necessary checks were carried out it was decided that I was suffering from angina. Many people live for many years with this complaint, which relieved both Tony and myself.

It meant I could go back to my promise to Mum and that was all that really mattered. I managed to come off all the pills by Christmas and from that time on I never looked back. I thanked White Arrow for his assistance for without his help I couldn't have done it.

Christmas, however, was terrible for all of us. It was the first one without Mum. We all tried hard to make the most of it, but we all had our minds on Mum. As I was able to see and hear Mum, perhaps it wasn't as bad for me, and I told the others that Mum wanted us to try and enjoy Christmas, but it wasn't the same.

On Christmas Day Tony asked if I wanted to go out for a drive. I felt down in the dumps, besides I had lost faith in my ability as a medium when it came to giving messages to clients from their loved ones in the spirit world. It was the first time I had ever questioned or doubted my working with spirit. They had always been right up until now so why should I be feeling like this? White Arrow soon picked up my train of thought and appeared on the back seat of the car. He showed no emotion at all in his face.

'Little One,' he said, 'remember this. All you are to me is an instrument. What I tell you, you say. If you are losing your confidence that's your hard luck, but there are people who need the spirit world to help them and that is my work – to help them. I know you have suffered in the past weeks, but you cannot let others suffer because of your pain.'

He was very abrupt and to the point, and with that, he vanished.

My first thought was, 'And a merry Christmas to you, too!' but then I realised he was right. I was being selfish and wallowing in my own self-pity.

He certainly chosen the right words. They pulled me out of the doldrums. At long last I now accepted that it was my mother's destiny to die at that time. Although in a sense I had known it all along, I wouldn't accept it until that Christmas Day's afternoon drive. I went back to work after the holiday, not giving one hundred per cent any more, but one hundred and fifty per cent. I had been made to see I was not the only one with worries and grief to contend with, and it took White Arrow's cutting me down to size to make me see sense and I'm truly thankful to God that I was privileged to be able to see Mum in spirit form.

Gradually, as time went by, the pain got easier. I was still missing her living presence, but I was so grateful that I could still communicate with her in spirit. My work with White Arrow got busier and I loved helping the people through him. Working with White Arrow I learnt so many things, but most of all I learnt to care for other people. My experiences of the past had made me realise how important it was for me to have gone through it all, for without the hell I had been through how could I possibly understand their anxieties and troubles? No problem seemed too big or too small for White Arrow and the greatest joy of all, up to this present day, is seeing the end result. I am always at my happiest when working with for the spirit world. I am working towards a perfect world, and I know that where the spirits are, that is heaven.

There are so many stories I would tell you about White Arrow and the spirit world, but my purpose in writing this book is not to tell you of the wonderful things the spirit can do through me, but the wonderful things that *your* guides and your families can do for you. After your sitting with a medium, your guides and families carry on performing the miracles for you.

As I sit here, writing my last few lines, I look back over the years and can remember what I have learnt through White Arrow's teachings. He told me once that on earth we all have a pathway to live and that at times it would very likely be like sheer hell to us, but before we pass on to spirit, that is, return to heaven where we lived before coming to earth, we should not try to return to spirit before our allotted time, for then we would only have to return to earth again to learn the same painful lessons all over again. I have thought about the times I had wanted to leave this earth in the hope of finding happiness in heaven, but then I looked at White Arrow and said, 'No, heaven can come later,' and for the first time I was pleased I was here.

White Arrow winked at me and I knew he understood, and I knew that whatever was in store for me, I could make it with him by my side.

Sister-Medicine Bear Woman:

I have some great news to tell you, remember that lady I was telling you about – Reba Ogle. She was telling me that she really enjoyed your book and that she could relate to it, and what really surprised her the most was that she knew 'WHITE FEATHER' who is in her family background, of which she found out a while back when she was looking through the Tribal Archives. Reba came back to my office and told me that she somehow feels connected to you and listen to this she said that she may have some white blood in her, because she remembers her grandma telling her that long ago in the 1800's the Sioux found a little white girl where the wagons were burning and everyone was killed off except for this little white girl. The Sioux took her and raised her like their own and yes she married a Indian warrior, and yes 'WHITE FEATHER' is related to White Eagles and also to RED EAGLES and this is Reba maiden name, she would be a relative to White Feather. So now she is going to go back to the Tribal Archives and see if she can get more information on White Feather. I told her that you wanted to get a family history for White Feather or White Arrow. So I am just excited about this that I just had to write to you and YES Reba wants to meet with you in person, I told her that you might come to the states this summer or next summer and that I would let her know.

Well, I hope that this news thrills both you and White Arrow ... and yes they are connected to 'Sitting Bull' somehow and this she had to look up too in the Tribal Records/Archives. I am just so amazed at all this ... Well I have to bring this letter to a close, because I have to get back to work now, my boss keeps walking by my office and I better go now. Take care and May the Creator watch and Bless you and your family. Tell White Arrow Hello and I am still waiting ...

Your Sister
Red Blossom Woman